Preface

A fro-Brazilians: Time for Recognition is a balanced, cogently argued call for action and for change, a call which is growing louder and louder. It is hoped that this Report – like MRG's earlier publications (Dzidzienyo and Casal, 1979; MRG, 1995) – will help to raise awareness of the issues facing people of African descent in Brazil today.

This new Report is published by Minority Rights Group International (MRG) to coincide with the 500th anniversary of the arrival of the Portuguese in Brazil. Most Afro-Brazilians will not be joining in the 'celebrations' to mark the event. Throughout the year 2000 and beyond, many people will be questioning how far Brazil has come and how far it has to go to meet the needs and aspirations of all its citizens. Afro-Brazilians are using the occasion to draw attention to the discrimination which they continue to experience.

The author of Afro-Brazilians: Time for Recognition, Dr Darien J. Davis, is a highly respected writer and historian on Latin American issues and on Afro-Brazilians in particular. In this new Report, Dr Davis outlines one of the central dilemmas facing modern-day Brazil: how is it that Afro-Brazilians have shaped so much of Brazilian culture yet remain politically and economically disenfranchised?

This discrimination is such that MRG will be seeking to raise the many issues contained in this Report at the forthcoming World Conference on Racism. The Report clearly describes how skin pigmentation is still used generally to delineate a social hierarchy within Brazil. It discusses the fact that Afro-Brazilians, while thought by many to form a numerical majority in Brazil, are discriminated against at almost every level of Brazilian life. Infant mortality is almost a third higher for Afro-Brazilians than for other Brazilians, in rural areas Afro-Brazilians are frequently among the landless, Afro-Brazilians' access to education is extremely poor, discrimination in employment is rife and police violence towards Afro-Brazilians – and Afro-Brazilian children and young men in particular – is commonplace.

Yet the myth of Brazil as a 'racial democracy' remains a potent one. Afro-Brazilians: Time for Recognition seeks to expose this myth and challenge the stereotypes of Afro-Brazilian women and men which abound. In their place, the Report seeks to depict the everyday reality of many Afro-Brazilians' lives. For while discrimination is a feature of almost all Afro-Brazilians' experience, Afro-Brazilians are far from a homogeneous group and should not be treated as such.

While calling for change, MRG recognizes and celebrates the work of many Afro-Brazilian organizations which are raising awareness of the many issues and campaigning to inform people of their rights. MRG has itself provided training and supported an internship for a worker for the Brazilian NGO, Geledés. MRG also recognizes that Brazil is not unique among Latin American countries in discriminating against people of African descent, that it has an exemplary record of ratification of international human rights standards and that its 1988 Constitution contains numerous safeguards for the rights of all its citizens. This Report calls for the full implementation of all these rights and for the recognition of the value of diversity within Brazil. To this end, MRG's Report concludes with a set of recommendations seeking to end the discrimination against Afro-Brazilians and to ensure their right to full participation in all aspects of Brazilian life.

Alan Phillips
Director
December 1999

Introduction and background

With the beginning of the new millennium, Brazil and Portugal will celebrate the quincentenary of the 'discovery' of Brazil by Pedro Alvares Cabral in 1500. Much of the celebration will focus on the technological innovations of the Portuguese, the transfer of Portuguese culture to the new world, and the Portuguese role in the genesis of a new people – the Brazilians. Cabral's landing in Brazil began a process of cultural intermingling among Portuguese, indigenous peoples and Africans which created the basis of modern Brazil. For many, however, the quincentenary presents an opportune moment for reflection on the consequences of colonization for the land and peoples whom the Portuguese subdued and forced into bondage. The dispersed regional economies of colonial Brazil first relied on the forced labour of the indigenous peoples, and later on slaves uprooted from the African continent. The presence of millions of Africans and their descendants in Brazil – once one of the 'greatest slave economies of human history'[1] – touched every aspect of Brazilian society.

This report aims to examine the legacy of those African slaves, and the current position of their descendants, in an attempt to understand how and why Africans were able to influence and shape Brazilian culture so profoundly yet still remain politically and economically disenfranchised after 500 years. In 1988, the year which marked the centenary of Brazil's abolition of slavery, Ana Maria Guimarães, the then 18-year-old Miss Pernambuco beauty queen, remarked that the only difference between South Africa and Brazil was that in Brazil 'white people don't kill you'. Since 1988, South Africa has reformed its political and economic system and the black majority wields substantial power. What has happened in Brazil? To understand the answer to this question, we must first look at four other questions:

1. Who are the Afro-Brazilians and how have they contributed to the development of Brazilian society?

2. How have they been marginalized (and how do they continue to be marginalized) from mainstream Brazilian society?

3. What have Afro-Brazilians and their allies done to combat their disenfranchisement?

4. What prospects do Afro-Brazilians have in the future?

To answer these questions, it is necessary to place the Afro-Brazilian struggle within the context of Brazilian national economic and political developments since 1500.

Brazil, the largest country in Latin America, is an immense territory of approximately 8.5 million square kilometres, divided into 26 distinct states and the federal district. Historically, Brazilians have been regionalist, having first been divided into *captaincies*, which were conquered territories extending from the coast into the interior. The Portuguese Crown sold captaincies to Portuguese entrepreneurs, known as *captain generals*, who were responsible for their economic development, and who exercised almost complete political control over the territories for much of the colonial period.

Despite the regionalism, it is possible to talk in general about 'Afro-Brazilians', a term whose Portuguese equivalent *'Afro-brasileiro'* is not universally used in Brazil. Brazilians often employ the term *'Afro-brasileiro'* to refer to types of Brazilian cultural productions with significant African influence, or to groups of people who claim African identity, but rarely use it to refer to themselves or others on an individual basis. More common is reference to skin colour. Descriptive characterizations of people's skin colour (light skin, dark, etc.) is typical of many South American communities with large populations of African descent. And in Brazil the elite have historically used differences among people of African descent as a means to dominate them.

Depending on region, Brazilians may refer to themselves as *branco* (white), *negro* or *preto* (black), or *indígena* (indigenous). While these categories might seem more or less clear, they are not since an individual might use any of the above terms to refer either to their colour (pigmentation) or the race to which they believe they belong. Then there are a number of categories used to refer to complexion or pigmentation, biological identity, or hair colour such as *mulato*[2] (the biological product of a white and black couple, light-skinned), *moreno* (brown-skinned, dark hair, tanned, etc.), *cafuso* (offspring of a black and indigenous couple, or looking like such a mixture, but also a dark-skinned mulatto with straight hair) and *caboclo* (indigenous, or copper-toned), to describe a few.

The use of *negro* and *negra* to refer to someone's race regardless of skin colour is increasingly common however, perhaps as a result of heightened racial consciousness and solidarity. This report will use the terms Afro-Brazilian and *negro* (or black) interchangeably to refer to *pretos*, mulattos and *afro-mestiços*, that is all people of African ancestry, whether mixed with European, indigenous or other ancestry. Where this is not possible the terms *mulatos* or *afro-mestiços*, or the official government near-equivalent term, *pardo*, will be used.

A worker takes a break.
Marcella Haddad

Afro-Brazilians: Time for Recognition

CONTENTS

BY DARIÉN J DAVIS

Declaration on the Rights of Persons Belonging to National or Ethnic, Religious or Linguistic Minorities (Adopted by General Assembly Resolution 47/135 of 18 December 1992)

Article 1

1. States shall protect the existence and the national or ethnic, cultural, religious and linguistic identity of minorities within their respective territories and shall encourage conditions for the promotion of that identity.
2. States shall adopt appropriate legislative and other measures to achieve those ends.

Article 2

1. Persons belonging to national or ethnic, religious and linguistic minorities (hereinafter referred to as persons belonging to minorities) have the right to enjoy their own culture, to profess and practise their own religion, and to use their own language, in private and in public, freely and without interference or any form of discrimination.
2. Persons belonging to minorities have the right to participate effectively in cultural, religious, social, economic and public life.
3. Persons belonging to minorities have the right to participate effectively in decisions on the national and, where appropriate, regional level concerning the minority to which they belong or the regions in which they live, in a manner not incompatible with national legislation.
4. Persons belonging to minorities have the right to establish and maintain their own associations.
5. Persons belonging to minorities have the right to establish and maintain, without any discrimination, free and peaceful contacts with other members of their group and with persons belonging to other minorities, as well as contacts across frontiers with citizens of other States to whom they are related by national or ethnic, religious or linguistic ties.

Article 3

1. Persons belonging to minorities may exercise their rights, including those set forth in the present Declaration, individually as well as in community with other members of their group, without any discrimination.
2. No disadvantage shall result for any person belonging to a minority as the consequence of the exercise or non-exercise of the rights set forth in the present Declaration.

Article 4

1. States shall take measures where required to ensure that persons belonging to minorities may exercise fully and effectively all their human rights and fundamental freedoms without any discrimination and in full equality before the law.
2. States shall take measures to create favourable conditions to enable persons belonging to minorities to express their characteristics and to develop their culture, language, religion, traditions and customs, except where specific practices are in violation of national law and contrary to international standards.
3. States should take appropriate measures so that, wherever possible, persons belonging to minorities may have adequate opportunities to learn their mother tongue or to have instruction in their mother tongue.
4. States should, where appropriate, take measures in the field of education, in order to encourage knowledge of the history, traditions, language and culture of the minorities existing within their territory. Persons belonging to minorities should have adequate opportunities to gain knowledge of the society as a whole.
5. States should consider appropriate measures so that persons belonging to minorities may participate fully in the economic progress and development in their country.

Article 5

1. National policies and programmes shall be planned and implemented with due regard for the legitimate interests of persons belonging to minorities.
2. Programmes of cooperation and assistance among States should be planned and implemented with due regard for the legitimate interests of persons belonging to minorities.

Article 6

States should cooperate on questions relating to persons belonging to minorities, inter alia, exchanging information and experiences, in order to promote mutual understanding and confidence.

Article 7

States should cooperate in order to promote respect for the rights set forth in the present Declaration.

Article 8

1. Nothing in the present Declaration shall prevent the fulfilment of international obligations of States in relation to persons belonging to minorities. In particular, States shall fulfil in good faith the obligations and commitments they have assumed under international treaties and agreements to which they are parties.
2. The exercise of the rights set forth in the present Declaration shall not prejudice the enjoyment by all persons of universally recognized human rights and fundamental freedoms.
3. Measures taken by States to ensure the effective enjoyment of the rights set forth in the present Declaration shall not prima facie be considered contrary to the principle of equality contained in the Universal Declaration of Human Rights.
4. Nothing in the present Declaration may be construed as permitting any activity contrary to the purposes and principles of the United Nations, including sovereign equality, territorial integrity and political independence of States.

Article 9

The specialized agencies and other organizations of the United Nations system shall contribute to the full realization of the rights and principles set forth in the present Declaration, within their respective fields of competence.

International Convention on the Elimination of All Forms of Racial Discrimination

(Adopted by the UN General Assembly Resolution 2106 (XX) of 21 December 1965)

Article 2

2. States Parties shall, when the circumstances so warrant, take, in the social economic, cultural and other fields, special and concrete measures to ensure the adequate development and protection of certain racial groups or individuals belonging to them, for the purpose of guaranteeing them the full and equal enjoyment of human rights and fundamental freedoms. These measures shall in no case entail as a consequence the maintenance of unequal or separate rights for different racial groups after the objectives for which they were taken have been achieved.

Convention on the Rights of the Child

(Adopted by the UN General Assembly Resolution 44/25 of 20 November 1989)

Article 6

1. States Parties recognize that every child has the inherent right to life.
2. States Parties shall ensure to the maximum extent possible the survival and development of the child.

Article 30

In those States in which ethnic, religious or linguistic minorities or persons of indigenous origin exist, a child belonging to such a minority or who is indigenous shall not be denied the right, in community with other members of his or her group, to enjoy his or her own culture, to profess and practise his or her own religion, or to use his or her own language.

Article 44

1. States Parties undertake to submit to the Committee, through the Secretary-General of the United Nations, reports on the measures they have adopted which give effect to the rights recognized herein and on the progress made on the enjoyment of those rights:
(a) Within two years of the entry into force of the Convention for the State Party concerned;
(b) Thereafter every five years.

International Covenant on Civil and Political Rights

(Adopted by the UN General Assembly Resolution 2200A (XXI) of 16 December 1966)

Article 2

3. Each State Party to the present Covenant undertakes:
(a) To ensure that any person whose rights or freedom as herein recognized are violated shall have an effective remedy, notwithstanding that the violation has been committed by persons acting in an official capacity;
(b) To ensure that any person claiming such a remedy shall have his right hereto determined by competent judicial, administrative or legislative authorities, or by any other competent authority provided for by the legal system of the State and to develop the possibilities of judicial remedy;
(c) To ensure that the competent authorities shall enforce such remedies when granted.

Article 6

1. Every human being has the inherent right to life. This right shall be protected by law. No one shall be arbitrarily deprived of his life.

Article 27

In those States in which ethnic, religious or linguistic minorities exist, persons belonging to such minorities shall not be denied the right, in community with the other members of their group, to enjoy their own culture, to profess and practise their own religion, or to use their own language.

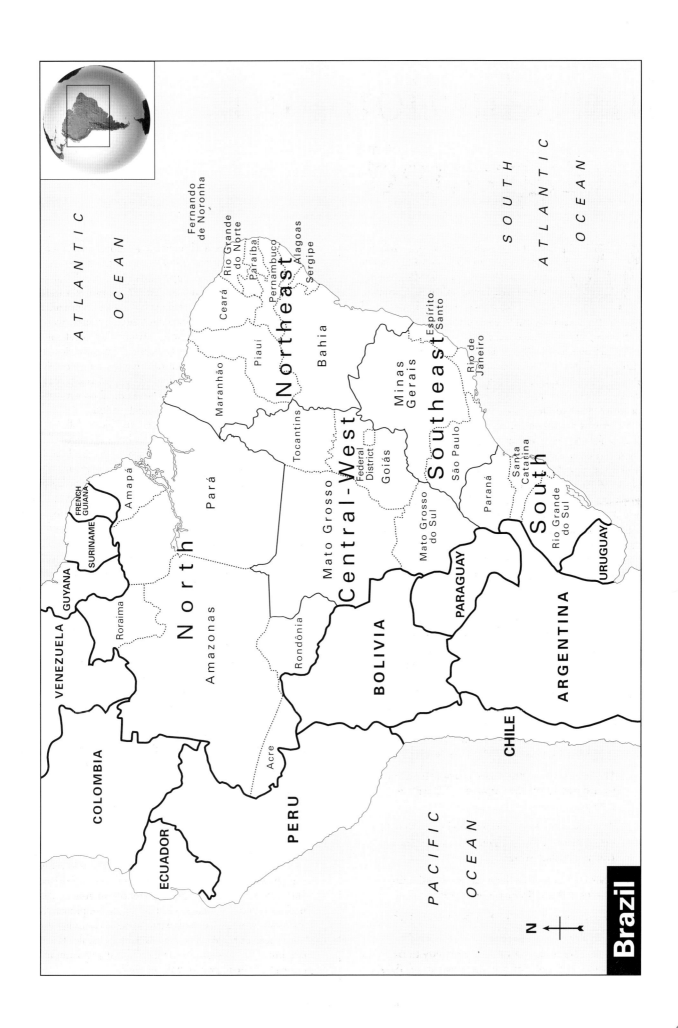

ATLANTIC OCEAN

SOUTH ATLANTIC OCEAN

Fernando de Noronha

Rio Grande do Norte

Paraíba

Pernambuco

Alagoas

Sergipe

Ceará

Piauí

Maranhão

Bahia

Northeast

Espírito Santo

Minas Gerais

Rio de Janeiro

Tocantins

Central-West

Federal District

Goiás

Southeast

São Paulo

Amapá

Pará

North

Santa Catarina

Paraná

South

Rio Grande do Sul

URUGUAY

Roraima

Mato Grosso

Mato Grosso do Sul

FRENCH GUIANA

SURINAME

Amazonas

Rondônia

PARAGUAY

GUYANA

VENEZUELA

Acre

BOLIVIA

ARGENTINA

COLOMBIA

PERU

CHILE

ECUADOR

PACIFIC OCEAN

N

Brazil

5

Afro-Brazilians and their contributions to Brazilian culture: the outsiders inside

The historical literature on Africans and their descendants in Brazil covers three broad themes: (1) the machinations of the institution of slavery, (2) accommodation of Africans to the New World, and (3) African resistance to Portuguese slavery and colonization. Of the three, the last has proved particularly challenging for historians. The African experience in Brazil has been diverse. Many enslaved and freed Africans and Afro-Brazilians worked within the Portuguese political system, contributing to economic, social and cultural developments. Others resisted Portuguese authority, preserving African customs and traditions outside the framework of Portuguese domination.

Today, many Brazilians believe that Afro-Brazilians do not appreciate their cultural roots, but few realize how profoundly colonization affected many Brazilians' views of their national culture. Throughout history, many white and black people shared a lack of appreciation for Brazilian culture in general, looking towards Europe, particularly France and Great Britain, for validation. Despite the importance of the African contribution to society, the Brazilian elite has systematically attempted to ignore Brazil's African-ness. The Brazilian state has also historically downplayed racial conflict, often describing the Afro-Brazilian position in society favourably in relation to that of slaves in the United States, or workers and peasants in Europe.

A careful reading of Brazilian history will indicate, to paraphrase the book edited by Emanoel Araújo, the Afro-Brazilian artist and current director of the Pinacoteca Estadual, São Paulo's main museum, that the Afro-Brazilian handprint is almost everywhere.[3] How ironic, as Gilberto Gil, the Afro-Brazilian singer and songwriter put it, that black people have been stereotypically portrayed throughout history as dirty and lazy when it was African men and women and their descendants who cleaned up the waste and dirt of the Portuguese.[4] Afro-Brazilians were also responsible for much of the cultural production of the colonial era, both sacred and profane. Afro-Brazilian lay brotherhoods and sisterhoods created images, statues, architectural designs and musical compositions for many Catholic religious establishments. The works of Afro-Brazilian artists such as Manoel da Cunha, the eighteenth-century painter from Rio de Janeiro, and Antonio Francisco Lisboa the eighteenth-century sculptor known popularly as Alejadinho, are vivid reminders of that legacy.

African resistance took many different forms, from religious and cultural resistance, to sabotage on plantations, to runaway slave communities, known as *mocambos* or *quilombos*. According to R.K. Kent, there were three basic forms of active resistance by slaves: fugitive slave settlements … attempts at seizures of power, and armed insurrections which neither sought escape nor control, but amelioration'.[5] Many Africans were able to buy their freedom, but because of lack of mobility and access to other sources of livelihood they were still at the mercy of the master. Records indicate that women were freed twice as often as men, and that males had their best chance of manumission as children or old men. Women performed a number of economic and social functions (as cooks, street vendors, prostitutes, etc.), and white masters often maintained their relationships with them once they were freed thus continuing to profit from their work.

Both men and women escaped from Portuguese settlements to struggle actively against Portuguese dominance, however.[6] The most celebrated example of slave resistance in the colonial period was the kingdom of Palmares (1603–94/5).[7] A combination of many *quilombos* joining together, Palmares was a complex dynamic system which survived for almost a century. Life within the escaped slave communities was subject to various influences due to Brazilian geography, the slaves' separation from Africa, the presence of indigenous peoples in the hinterland, and the amount of acculturation that the slaves had already undergone under the Portuguese.[8] As Richard Price notes, escaped slave societies dotted the map of Brazil, from the forest to the interior (where they often merged with bands of indigenous people), to the outskirts of major urban centres.[9] The Portuguese succeeded in destroying Palmares in 1695, but throughout the pre-abolition era, *quilombos* rose up again and again. Since abolition in 1888, Palmares has become an inspiration for men and women all over Brazil. In recent years, 20 November, the date of the death of one of Palmares' greatest leaders, Zumbi, has become an important day for the celebration of Afro-Brazilian culture and a display of Afro-Brazilian solidarity.

Afro-Brazilian religions and African languages

While Portuguese dominance ensured that African elements of culture and language would be subjugated, it could not eliminate them. African elements survived in *quilombos* as well as through cultural mixing with Portuguese and indigenous elements. Thus the African cultural imprint on Brazilian culture is not monolithic. Many different African customs from a number of African ethnic groups underwent changes through contact with one another and the surrounding context. African customs are present in almost every aspect of Brazilian culture today, especially in language and religion.

The Portuguese language in Brazil is distinct from the language spoken in Portugal as Brazilian Portuguese adapted both to indigenous speakers, acquiring indigenous terms and expressions, and to a number of African languages and dialects. Yoruba words and expressions are noticeable in the Northeast, especially in Bahian cooking terms and the prayers and songs which constitute part of the *Candomblé* religion. Yoruba religious terms have seeped into mainstream parlance and most Brazilians understand words of Yoruba origin such as *orixá* and *axé*.

According to Afro-Brazilian writer and scholar Nei Lopes, while the Yoruba language was more present in relation to food and religions, the languages commonly known as Bantu, a word coined in 1862 by a German philologist to refer a group of languages spoken from Cameroon to Tanzania, had a more pervasive impact on Brazilian Portuguese. Close research and comparison with Bantu languages from Africa reveals not just similarities in words, but in the use of words. Words such as *fubá* (corn meal), *mocambo* (escaped slave community), *samba* and *maxixe* (Brazilian dances) come directly from Bantu languages. Kicongo, Umbundu and Kimbundu are three of the most common Bantu languages which influenced Brazil. Anthropologists have registered other African languages in remote corners of Brazil such as Catumbá, Minas Gerais and Cafuná, São Paulo, although their influence is not as pervasive as that of Bantu or Yoruba.[10]

Africans left an indelible mark on Catholicism, but Africans also transferred intact their belief systems and visions of morality and the afterlife, often adopting a façade of Catholic symbols and images. This is evident in the practice of many Afro-Brazilian religions such as *Candomblé*. While some believers continue to associate *Candomblé* deities or *orixás* with Catholic saints, for others this association ceases to exist in an era when persecution has diminished.

Derived from the Yoruba people of West Africa, *Candomblé* seeks harmony with nature. The religion is organized around religious centres known as *terreiros*, which are usually led by high priestesses, *mãe de santos* (mother of saints) or priests, *pai de santos* (father of saints). Followers worship a pantheon of *orixás* in an annual cycle, like the liturgical cycle of the Catholic Church. While *orixás* are more powerful than human beings they are not necessarily more moral. Each deity represents a given force or element in nature, and has a favourite colour and type of food. Yemanja, for example, is the goddess of the sea, who usually dresses in blue and white. The favourite colour of Oxun, the goddess of beauty, is yellow. In the religious ceremonies, practitioners dress in the colours of the *orixás* and place food at the altar before singing specific songs and dancing precisely choreographed steps to the sacred drums. The anthropomorphic nature of the *orixá* allows an intimate contact between believer and deity, and the highlight of the *Candomblé* ceremony is the epiphany, or possession, when the *orixá* takes over the believer's body.

Umbanda is more Brazilianized than *Candomblé*. *Umbanda*, which developed in Brazil in the 1920s, has elements of African religions, Christianity, indigenous rites and beliefs and other spiritist beliefs. *Umbanda* is practised mostly in the urban areas of the South and Southeast. Other religions have developed syncretically with Catholicism, or in some cases with indigenous rites such as *Candomblé-de-caboclo*, also known in Bahia as *Religião de caboclo*. A number of other African-based religions can be found in the Northeast (*Xangó*) and in the South (*Preto-minas*). Followers of *Batuque* in Belém in the North refer to their deities as *encantados*.

Historically, women have played important roles in Afro-Brazilian religions. Indeed, across all religions, the census data suggests that more women declare allegiance to religion than men. Compared to other religions, however, women actually wield substantial authority in Afro-Brazilian religions such as *Candomblé*. *Candomblé* priestesses in Bahia such as the legendary Mãe Menininha do Gantois, Mãe Stela and Mãe Hilda are well known and respected outside of their religious communities.

→ moment of sudden + great revelation

The evolution of civil rights

The struggle of Africans, Afro-Brazilians and progressive elements of Brazilian white society led to the abolition of slavery in 1888, when the Golden Law of 13 May was signed by Princess Isabel, the daughter of the reigning monarch Pedro II. After abolition, Afro-Brazilians campaigned for social integration and recognition but were often blocked by overriding national concerns and official and unofficial censorship. The exact dynamics, however, varied considerably from region to region. Nonetheless, examining the status of civil rights on a national scale through six distinct historical periods – (1) slavery (1822–88); (2) post-abolition (1888–1930); (3) the Second Republic, the Vargas years (1930–44); (4) transitional democracy (1944–64); (5) military dictatorship (1964–79); and (6) the political opening (1979–85) – can help in understanding the social, political and cultural dynamics which shaped civil and racial discourses today.

These six periods forged distinct visions of Brazilian reality and a national discourse within which the discourse of civil rights and racial consciousness emerged. Afro-Brazilians did not develop a civil rights movement comparable to that of the United States because of Brazil's unique historical development, which produced different patterns of social interaction. Brazil's Catholic corporatist culture, and its unique political and economic patterns of organization, gave rise to a system that was unjust and which institutionalized white privilege, although a number of Afro-Brazilians, particularly mulattos, were able to secure economic and social advantages within the system. Moreover, Africans and their descendants in Brazil were able to preserve many of their customs and cultural traits in ways not possible in North America. But this resulted from the structural nature of Brazilian colonization, not from any benevolence on the part of the Portuguese.

For much of the twentieth century, the Brazilian state's nationalist rhetoric, which encouraged identification with a national family, prohibited the emergence of strong racial consciousness, a process which is necessary for the preservation of minority rights. In the absence of a democratic civil society (because of the monarchy, the Vargas dictatorship and the military dictatorship), official channels of discourse were often closed to Afro-Brazilians as well as to other sectors of civil society. A number of factors, including ignorance of civil rights, lack of education, misinformation about the law and general disenfranchisement inherited from the patriarchal and racist colonial tradition, render politics and activities in the public domain off limits to most Brazilians, but particularly to Afro-Brazilians and the indigenous peoples. This, together with precarious economic conditions, which have denied and continue to deny more than three-quarters of the population access to economic and cultural opportunities and consequently the legal system, historically have made it difficult for Afro-Brazilians to speak of civil rights. Afro-Brazilian activists have more often framed their struggles in terms of human rights.[11]

The struggle for the rights of people of African descent in Brazil has developed over a period of more than 100 years, and only at the end of the twentieth century are small changes noticeable. The problems of the current movement and its prospects for success are necessarily shaped by its historical past. The extent to which Afro-Brazilians can overcome past challenges and re-state their preoccupations in a new political era will serve as a measure of their political power in the future. Today, more Afro-Brazilians are conscious of their civil rights than ever before, but many more remain politically, economically, socially and culturally disenfranchised. The current Brazilian Constitution is the most precise document vis-a-vis racial and ethnic discrimination that Brazil has ever had, but Afro-Brazilians' continued participation in the country's political and economic processes is essential to safeguard and protect their rights.

Slavery (1822–88)

Prior to abolition, politicians debated the advantages and disadvantages of maintaining the system of African bondage. Brazilian activists campaigned to change society's perception and treatment of slaves, appealing to citizens' sense of justice and using both moral and economic arguments. But unlike many North American abolitionists, such as John Rankin,[12] whose morality argument implied the immediate freeing of the slave, Brazilians advocated a gradual process: abolition of the trade in 1851, the Free Womb Law in 1871, the Sexagenarian Law of 1885 and finally abolition in 1888. Parliament instituted all these laws under the monarchist Constitution that dated back to 1824.[13]

Essential to many abolitionists' stand against slavery was the hope of the whitening process, the wish for Brazil to become more European. As Joaquim Nabuco, one of Brazil's best-known abolitionists noted, 'We must abolish slavery because it continues to repel potential European immigration.'[14] Nabuco likewise opposed Asian immigration, as it would 'complicate the situation'.[15] Nabuco's status as advocate for slave's rights is nonetheless undisputed.

He argued that slaves had a right to freedom as 'creators of Brazil', setting a precedent for what would later become the myth of 'racial democracy', the idea that racial barriers to social mobility did not operate in Brazil.[16]

Many free Afro-Brazilians participated in the abolitionist campaign, among them the journalist José Carlos do Patrocínio (1854–1905), André Rebouças (1838–98) and Luis Gonzaga de Pinto Gama (1830–82). One year after abolition, the monarchy was dismantled and Brazil became a republic. Prior to 1888, many slave-owners had manumitted their slaves, as had many communities and states. Ceará and Amazonas, for example, declared all slaves free in 1884. A number of communities in Rio Grande do Sul followed this example. Not all slave-owners in these communities freed their slaves, but people of conscience began to set a standard before a law mandated action.[17]

Post-abolition (1888–1930)

Slaves are not mentioned in the Constitution that governed Brazil from 1824 to 1891. The 'Guarantee of Political and Civil Rights of Brazilian Citizens', Title XIII, Article 173–9, assures Brazilians of both liberty and the right to property. Slaves were considered property and were treated as such.[18] The political and legal system continued to ignore the slaves after abolition and the creation of the republic. Republicanism assumed a high degree of mobility among the population, proposed an education programme and limited the role of the Church. Modelled after that of the United States of America, the republican Constitution of 21 February 1891 formed the framework for government in Brazil until 1934.[19]

The republican Constitution reiterated the rights of Brazilian citizens to liberty, security and property. All were supposedly equal under the law, but the mobility of ex-slaves was limited by the liberal oligarchy. Lack of general education in the population at large, a Constitution with ill-defined individual rights and an authoritarian capitalist model of development which valued property above individual rights, weakened civil rights. Brazil began to industrialize without breaking down the framework and attitudes of pre-abolition society. The state regarded social questions as a matter for the police.[20]

The military had become one of the most prestigious national institutions following the War of Paraguay in 1864.[21] 'Positivism', a conservative ideology which emerged out of liberalism, pervaded state thinking. Positivists called for reform within a paternalistic, hierarchical framework which valued order above all.[22] According to the Brazilian scholar, Gilberto Freyre, the emerging middle classes embraced positivism precisely because of its conservatism and emphasis on order. Although debates on the merits of immigration often divided positivists, the official position of the state was to move away from ex-slave labour and to promote European immigration, a move that many hoped would 'whiten' the population.[23]

The Brazilian elite called for the assimilation of the ex-slaves and protection of the indigenous population. The positivists in the government spearheaded the drive for the creation of Brazil's Indian Service (1910) which aimed to preserve indigenous peoples' culture and lands,

for example.[24] They believed that people were capable of evolving from an 'inferior position' to a 'superior one', and that ex-slaves, now citizens, would eventually be assimilated into mainstream Brazilian society.[25] Little social legislation was introduced to ensure that ex-slaves would be integrated into mainstream society, however, and Brazilians' desire to avoid discussion of slaves was demonstrated by Rui Barbosa's decree ordering the destruction of all records of slavery, to avoid any lingering stigma. Not all records were destroyed, but census and other types of demographic information on Afro-Brazilians are difficult to come by. The Brazilian elite continued to fear the masses well into the twentieth century.[26] The state lacked a concrete plan to integrate ex-slaves into society, a problem exacerbated by the presence of thousands of poor immigrants and indentured servants from Europe and Japan.

The Second Republic, the Vargas years (1930–44)

The political climate would not change until Getúlio Vargas' middle-class revolution of 1930 which initally benefited Afro-Brazilians. The Constitutional Assembly promulgated its Constitution on 16 June 1934, the most nationalistic constitutional document since independence in 1821. Among other national reforms, voting became obligatory, and women gained the right to vote.[27]

Title III of the Constitution, Chapter II ensured citizens' equality before the law, adding that:

> 'There will be no privileges, nor distinctions because of birth, sex, race, personal professions or professions of parents, social class, wealth, religious beliefs or political ideas.'[28]

Civil rights discourse took a decidedly non-confrontational line throughout this period. Nationalism and patriotism continued to define the limits of racial discourse from the 1930s until the 1980s. At the same time, the 1934 Constitution had adopted a decidedly anti-immigrant policy, establishing quotas to ensure 'ethnic integration'. This legislation, which was clearly aimed at Japanese immigrants, presents another example of the Brazilian state's overarching desire for conformity and ethnic homogeneity.[29]

Writers such as Gilberto Freyre examined the positive contributions of Africans to Brazilian society and began to encourage Brazilians to celebrate their African heritage – but as a contribution to a distinct Brazilian identity based on miscegenation and cultural intermingling. Freyre's contribution to civil rights was essentially in the educational realm, raising the historical consciousness of all Brazilians, yet he failed to note the victimization of black people and their limited social mobility. Indeed, Freyre had much in common with Brazilian intellectuals and artists in São Paulo, who began to call for a new way of seeing Brazil. These intellectuals, later known as the modernists, orchestrated a cultural nationalism within Brazil.[30] Many of this generation reinterpreted Brazil's past with a new appreciation of minorities within *brasilidade* or Brazilian-ness.

For many, Brazil could now project itself as a nation that had successfully blended elements of 'primitive cultures' with European elements. Brazil was a nation formed through the miscegenation of three major races, producing a magical union like no other place on earth. While President Vargas' regime (1930–44) resorted to repression of political dissenters who impeded national unification, Brazilian intellectuals began to explore and foster the myth of Brazil as a social paradise, which would later become known as *racial democracy*. This allowed upper-class (white) Brazilians to promulgate a mythical equality among the mulatto, *mestiço* and black sectors (the indigenous peoples still lived mostly in isolation). It also helped promote national consolidation and patriotism.

According to the American historian, Frank Tannenbaum: 'Many Brazilians will tell you that, in the future, the history of their country will be chronicled in two parts; that before and after Gilberto Freyre. The dividing line is [Freyre's] *Casa Grande e Senzala*... first published in 1933.'[31] The rapid miscegenation which Freyre saw seemed to bear out the theory of racial democracy, which implied that, regardless of racial background, all Brazilians had a basic social equality which allowed them to pursue their own, albeit limited, economic advantage.[32]

As Jean Franco has correctly observed, the Brazilian intellectuals of this period were too concerned with the national image. They ignored the subcultures, especially those of black people.[33] The effect of the modernist myths was the continued exclusion of black people from national life. Black people's representation in, and their importance to Brazilian national culture, was through assimilation. Thus many white people employed the mulatto to represent them, a phenomenon often referred to as the 'mulatto escape hatch', which is itself a myth: comparison of all the major socioeconomic indicators for black people and mulattos reveal similar and consistent characteristics, such as high unemployment and illiteracy rates, etc. compared to those of their white counterparts.

By the late 1930s the myth of racial democracy was taken for granted, despite earlier Brazilian efforts to attract white European immigrants, who had transformed the demographics of many Brazilian states, particularly those of the south. The strong ideology of whitening played a significant role in the continued marginalization of black people and mulattos – even as Brazilians continued to celebrate racial democracy. Whitening meant, first, that Brazil wanted to become a country of white people. If that could not be attained demographically then Brazil would project an image of whiteness. Thus most national representations, including in the areas of sports and music, where black people historically had more opportunities, would be white. Second, Brazilians celebrated miscegenation as a way for white people to absorb the black element into the white, and not necessarily as an indication of social equality.

The only civil rights legislation of this period came after the renowned Afro-North American entertainer Katherine Dunham was barred from entering a hotel in São Paulo,[34] an incident which attracted international attention. The name of Afonso Arinos de Melo Franco, an ardent supporter of national order, appears on the anti-discrimination legislation of 1951 that many Afro-Brazil-ians had been calling for since abolition. Ironically, during the period when Arinos was emphasizing an ideological agenda based on racial unity, two of Brazil's strongest racial movements emerged: the Frente Negra Brasileira (FNB) and the Teatro Experimental do Negro (TEN).

For the FNB, civil rights meant equal treatment under the law, the right to work free of discrimination and full integration of black people in national life. Its emergence in São Paulo in 1932 marked an important step in the national black consciousness movement within the Afro-Brazilian community, despite the conservative views of many of its leaders. By 1936, the FNB had registered as a political party, aiming to promote self-respect among black people and mulattos as well as instil 'working-class values' in its members. At its height the Frente Negra boasted a membership of over 200,000. Women of the FNB, known as *frente negrinhas*, played an important part, contributing to the education, self-esteem and care of black women.[35]

According to Florestan Fernandes, the most important change that the Frente brought to the black community was psychological, as the people began to change their self-concept regarding status and social roles. According to Francisco Lucrecio, secretary of the Frente from 1934 to 1937, the movement called for action within the black community rather than a protest against the white community. Indeed, the Frente praised the nationalist government of Getúlio Vargas.[36]

Ironically, it was Getúlio Vargas' dictatorship, known as the *Estado Novo* (New State) (1937–44), which abolished the FNB when all political organizations were declared illegal. While representing the culmination of Vargas' nationalist agenda to rid the country of socialism and fascism, like other South American governments of the time, Vargas promulgated one of the only two constitutions not written by a Constituent Assembly.[37] This Constitution guaranteed individual freedoms so long as peace, order and public security were maintained. Vargas relied on education to propagate his nationalism, issuing guidelines for compulsory physical education for the promotion of health, and civic education for the promotion of patriotism.[38] In the period 1934–7, most working-class Brazilians did not see an amelioration of their poor position vis-a-vis the upper classes, despite the intense industrialization and growth of the national infrastructure.[39]

Transitional democracy (1944–64)

When the *Estado Novo* ended in 1944, activists emerged, cautious in their political participation but ready to raise the standard on behalf of Afro-Brazilians. The new Constitution of 18 September 1946 brought a new legal framework. The bicameral legislature was re-instituted, the death penalty abolished and Chapter II, Article 141 provided the basis for individual rights to 'life, liberty, safety and personal property' while establishing that 'all are equal under the law'.[40]

While similar guarantees were written into previous Constitutions, the new environment of democracy engendered a sense of optimism and respect for the law that lasted until 1964. In this context, the Teatro Experimental do Negro (TEN) surfaced in 1944 with clearly defined objectives:

1. to educate Brazilians that there was no superior race nor was there natural servility, and to eliminate colour prejudice;

2. to propose policies that would enhance Afro-Brazilians' possibilities for education;

3. to combat racism following the code of conduct of the Brazilian Constitution which should properly define racial discrimination.[41]

The Teatro provided a forum for Afro-Brazilians to promote their civil rights, addressing specific issues such as cultural and economic discrimination. TEN argued that since abolition, persecution of Afro-Brazilian religion and disdain for African cultural influences had fostered an atmosphere which encouraged Brazilians to avoid a discussion of race relations.[42]

TEN called for its civil rights as human rights. In São Paulo, Porto Alegre and Santa Catarina, similar organizations arose with direct links to TEN.[43] In May 1949, along with several other Brazilian interest groups, TEN organized the First National Negro Congress to foster research on black issues. In an address to the Congress, Abdias do Nascimento, leader of the movement, pointed out that the channels for dissemination of information open to black people were inadequate. Furthermore, many black people organized around religious circles were being attacked by the state.[44]

TEN took part in the psychological polarization of Brazilian thought, aggressively pursuing the goal of consciousness-raising through literacy campaigns and putting out cultural information. Its members demanded proper treatment of all its citizens in politics, economics but especially in education. Despite the importance of education as mandated by the Constitution, Afro-Brazilians remained under-educated. Thus in a column in *Quilombo*, the newsletter of TEN, a student documented the discrimination against black children in the Brazilian school system. For example, black children had failed the military medical examinations as a result of blatant discrimination.[45] Indeed, the mere existence of TEN was a miracle as the Ministry of Education had failed to give the organization funding for their educational and literacy campaigns.[46]

TEN gave much energy and attention to the role of Afro-Brazilian women. One of the co-founders of TEN was the actress Ruth de Souza. María do Nascimento edited a column in *Quilombo*, dedicated to the woman's voice in Brazil. Topics covered ranged from the empowerment of domestics, who could influence upper-class children on how to be more socially tolerant, to features on important Afro-Brazilian women.[47] The Congresso Nacional das Mulheres Negras (National Congress of Black Women) was also established, and served as a centre mainly for professional women, domestic workers and female artists. The female section of TEN called for the integration of women of colour into social life. In the spirit of self-help, they ran a literacy campaign, a children's theatre for the education and recreation of children, and educational seminars for mothers.[48]

Military dictatorship (1964–79)

During the new democratic opening of the 1940s and 1950s, Afro-Brazilians began to use the ballot as a weapon in the struggle for their rights, supporting and working with other advocates outside of the movement.[49] However, the right-wing military coup of 1964 once again blocked Brazilian grassroots and social movements and weakened the country's democratic traditions. The 1967 Constitution, in part, reflected the spirit of the Constitution of 1937 in its authoritarian style, while including several of the gains of 1946. As a result of the work of many advocates in the 1940s and 1950s, prejudice was introduced as a national offence. The Constitution declared that: 'racial prejudice will be punished by law',[50] but prejudice remained ill-defined. Moreover, how would prejudice be punished? The military was more preoccupied with economic issues and maintaining social order.

In 1968, President Costa Silva succeeded Castelo Branco, the chief military officer behind the 1964 coup, but soon fell ill. A military junta handed presidential power to General Medici, beginning a period of corruption and unprecedented torture and persecution of 'subversives' from all classes. The military government created the Serviço Nacional de Informacão (National Information Service) and utilized the Departamento Autó nomo de Ordem Política e Social (Autonomous Department of Political and Social Order, known as DOPS), a government not-so-secret service responsible for weeding out 'subversives'. Subversion was loosely defined as challenges to the government. Medici and his successor, General Geisel, governed Brazil during the period known as the 'economic miracle'. Corruption and a strict military campaign for order filled the pockets of many military officials. Civil rights were virtually non-existent.

The 1969 Constitution reworded the civil rights law but definition remained problematic: 'racial prejudice will be punished by law'.[51] In the light of the suspension of habeas corpus in 1968, no rights were guaranteed.[52] Article 154 further restricted individual rights:

> *'The abuse of individual or political rights for subversive purposes against the democratic regime will result in the suspension of those rights for two to ten years to be determined by the Supreme Federal Tribunal.'*[53]

Military rule was a setback for grassroots and civil rights advocates who could be branded 'subversive' arbitrarily. How did advocates continue their work under this repressive framework? What discourse could challenge the status quo? Activists would have to find innovative ways, or they would have to frame their criticism within a nationalist framework.

The military regime of 1968 continued to promote nationalism along technocratic, scientific, cultural and other professional lines. This necessitated the creation of national research institutions. Inevitably, informed and independent advocates would emerge from academic circles. Florestan Fernandes was perhaps the most important of them. His book, *The Negro in Brazilian Society*, considered the classic work on race relations in Brazil, employs social science research methods to illustrate historic and continuing discrimination against Afro-Brazilians. Fernandes argued that Brazil's primary prejudice was the belief that there was no prejudice. He inspired a group of prominent social scientists interested in tackling Brazil's problems in the spirit of patriotism. Some of these academics, such as Fernando Henrique Cardoso and Octávio Ianni, became internationally known. Although Fernandes' focus was São Paulo, his work had national implications.[54]

Black people in urban areas such as São Paulo attracted a lot of attention when Brazil's military stressed industrialization as a key component of their modernization scheme. Modernization, and the emergence of a competitive social order, came slowly and did not eradicate the social class system to any significant extent. In fact, the capacity for social change was limited. To participate in the modernization process, Afro-Brazilians required material and psychological skills as well as technology which they currently lacked. Fernandes argued that Afro-Brazilians were handicapped because of the debasement of slavery, pauperism and their isolation through history.[55] He believed that social conditions would have to improve significantly for Afro-Brazilians in order for them to be integrated into the growing urban cultures.[56]

The political opening (1979–85)

Armed with empirical data produced by Fernandes and others, civil rights activists emerged in the period after the decline of the military. The worldwide oil crisis of the 1970s shocked the Brazilian military into reality. Much of the boom had been financed by borrowed money, while hard currency was siphoned off to pay for oil. Brazil's balance of payments suffered as corruption scandals proliferated. The military slowly began to relinquish its power. In 1979 General João Figueiredo presided over the period that would begin the political opening (*abertura*) or return to democracy, which culminated in the elections of 1985.[57] After a difficult process of political deliberation and debate and unprecedented mass civil mobilization, Brazil celebrated the creation of a new Constitution in 1988.

Afro-Brazilians did not wait for this, however. The political climate that allowed President Figueiredo to be elected on a promise to restore democracy motivated Afro-Brazilians, and a host of organizations emerged throughout the country. The newly felt presence of the Afro-Brazilian movement was seen with the celebration of the 'International Day for the Elimination of Racial Discrimination' on 21 March 1983 in Rio.[58] One important organization was the Movimento Negro Unificado, or MNU, which emerged in São Paulo in 1978. The MNU focused on many of the same issues as their predecessors: discrimination, prejudice and lack of jobs; but the 1980s brought new issues: police brutality, health care, battered women, the rights of children and the right to religious expression.[59]

The revision of the Brazilian Constitution that began in 1986 provided a national forum where activists could influence national law and attitudes concomitantly. Abdias do Nascimento, then the only Afro-Brazilian member of the National Congress, produced a list of demands, among others, that the Constitution define racism as a crime against humanity, institute mandatory literacy campaigns and guarantee racial compensations.[60]

While many of these demands were not met, the 1988 Constitution nonetheless represents a victory for civil rights activists. Article III set out the purpose of government: 'To ensure the good of all without prejudice of origin, race, sex, colour, age, or whatever other forms of discrimination.'[61] Title II, Article 5, pertaining to civil rights and liberties, was the most elaborate in the history of the Constitution. Part XLI mandated the punishment of discrimination: 'The law will punish any discrimination contrary to the law of fundamental rights and liberties.'[62] Part XLII clarifies the ambiguity of past Constitutions in relationship to discrimination: 'The practice of racism constitutes a crime … subject to imprisonment.'[63]

Afro-Brazilian activists participated enthusiastically throughout the constitutional reform, playing a significant role in the shaping of the anti-discrimination legislation. Since the 1930s the Afro-Brazilian activist community had grown into a diverse eclectic body, and many activists became viable candidates in the political process.[64] This phase of mobilization also saw a stronger alliance with progressive political elements and some activists. Two of the stronger parties were the Workers' Party or the Partido dos Trabalhadores (PT) and the Democratic Workers' Party, or the Partido Democrática Trabalhista (PDT). The penetration and alliance of political parties with various elements of the black movement would, on the one hand, allow for many black political candidates to be put forward; on the other, however, it fragmented the movement.[65]

Political candidates such as Otelino da Silva from Rio de Janeiro benefited from the political flexibility within the black movement. Da Silva promoted his ideas throughout the black community, speaking at organizations such as the Instituto das Pesquisas de Cultural Negras (Institute for Research on Black Culture, or IPCN). A member of the MNU, he ran for office in the new democratic Congress under the banner of the PDT. For Otelino, the PDT was the only organization that could politically represent the needs of the majority of Brazilians in the post-Cold War generation, with its motto: 'Peace, democracy and renovated socialism'. Otelino was a militant member of the MNU, but he stressed his alliance with all workers for the advancement of humanity.[66]

According to Paulo Roberto dos Santos, researcher for the Centro dos Estudos Afro-Asiáticos (Centre for Afro-Asiatic Studies), *abertura* (the opening) signified the major watershed of the Brazilian civil rights movement. Much of the consciousness-raising related to the national liberation of former Portuguese colonies such as Angola and Mozambique. Brazilians were also deeply affected by civil rights gains in North America. Groups emerging in the late 1970s and 1980s were characterized by ideological flexibility, political pluralism and commitment to activism and education. By 1985 more than 400 separate but related Afro-Brazilian organizations had emerged in different regions throughout the country.[67] Today there are more than 700 groups dedicated to the education, political, cultural and spiritual development of Afro-Brazilians.

In the states of São Paulo and Rio, more black people and mulattos have been appointed to top government positions since the late 1980s. Many more black people have gained access to universities and other institutions of higher learning. Yet Afro-Brazilians remain under-represented and the concept of civil or human rights in Brazil continues to be ill-defined, partly because the socioeconomic and political institutions are resistant to change. Surprisingly, many Brazilians still believe that prejudice does not exist in Brazil and think that many of the activists are racist because they focus only on the development of black people and not all Brazilians. Others acknowledge the importance of black people to the nation's past, but are unaware of their continued presence or their current struggle.

Contemporary Afro-Brazilian organizations and NGOs

The political *abertura* of the 1970s was an important watershed for the black movement in Brazil. The MNU surfaced at this time and attempted to bring together black people to voice their concerns about racial inequalities on a national level. Through demonstrations, political planning and networking, activists such as Lélia Gonzalez from the MNU in São Paulo and others associated with the IPCN in Rio, were instrumental in raising consciousness among thousands of black people throughout the country. By the mid-1980s, the MNU had branches in virtually all the Brazilian states, working alongside (and often at odds with) other local organizations. By the beginning of the 1990s, however, the strength of the MNU had diminished, in part because of factionalism and in part because Afro-Brazilians had begun to find other ways to voice their concerns, including through the federal, state and local government, political parties and independent NGOs. Thus, the black movement has grown into many diverse and eclectic bodies. The importance of the Afro-Brazilian activist movement in raising awareness among many Afro-Brazilians, including high-ranking officials such as Benedita da Silva, must not be underestimated. Nor should those Afro-Brazilian activists who now work for the government be chastised for accepting governmental positions, although those who have been coopted by policies which have not been beneficial to the community should be.

There are three main types of Afro-Brazilian organization: first, governmental entities and lobbies; second, national grassroots organizations; and third, regional NGOs which include independent social, political and cultural entities.

Governmental entities and lobbies

Black public officials are to be found throughout Brazil's 26 states and the federal district, but none have as much constitutional power and support from the federal authorities as the Fundacão Cultural Palmares (Palmares Cultural Foundation) for the black community.

The Fundação Cultural Palmares is a unique governmental organization and for that reason has a challenging role in the promotion of Afro-Brazilian civil rights. A part of the Ministry of Culture, with its seat in Brasília, the Fundação has played a pivotal role in the black community in the 1990s. A product of the 1988 Constitution, it was created as a result of demands from various sectors of the black movement. The foundation seeks to promote Afro-Brazilian cultural manifestations through research while also aiming to promote racial harmony and deter racial harassment, prejudice and discrimination. The foundation shares some goals with regional black organizations, although it has greater federal resources which allow it to sponsor events and support research on the contribution of Africans to Brazilian society.[68]

Perhaps the foundation's most important task to date has been its accreditation of *quilombos*, assisting their residents to attain title to their lands. The foundation is responsible for mapping and researching the *quilombos* to establish their legitimacy, in effect certifying them for approval of title. The foundation has often been criticized by activists for dragging its feet or for being inefficient, but it is under tremendous pressure from many groups while lacking the necessary tools, resources and staff to map the more than 700 official claims. Despite its drawbacks, the foundation does provide an important governmental channel previously unavailable to the black community.

While not exclusively concerned with the Afro-Brazilian communities, the Secretariat for Human Rights in Brasilia (directed by Ivar dos Santos) plays an important role nationally, along with a number of national branches of the United Nations (UNESCO, UNICEF, etc.). State human rights offices such as the Secretariat of Human Rights in Rio de Janeiro have relied upon the talents and militancy of black activists such as Abdias do Nascimento and Carlos Alberto Medeiros, a former aide to Edson Arantes do Nascimento (Pelé) at the Ministry of Sports. In Minas Gerais the state government has created a special Secretaria Municipal de Assuntos da Communidade Negra (Municipal Secretariat for Black Community Matters), directed by Diva Moreira, a woman with a long history of activism. São Paulo's Delegacia de Investigações sobre Crimes Raciais, a special police commission for investigating racial crimes, is an important centre for registering complaints and for providing services to victims of racial assaults. Other states are following this example, but a universal complaint of government officials is the lack of resources and the slow pace of change. Human rights or Afro-Brazilian organizations sanctioned by state or local governments have little power to change other branches of government or to enforce state or national laws.

National grassroots organizations

There are relatively few national organizations which are able to overcome the tremendous obstacles that inhibit grassroots cooperation across state lines. Some have managed to bring together resources to challenge collectively the status quo and specific government practices or national celebrations which ignore the plight of minorities. The Conselho Nacional de Entidades Negras (National Council of Black Entities, or CONEN) brings together groups from all over the country to discuss ways to pursue mutual support and to advance the black movement agenda on a national level. Members do not necessarily share a given ideology, or even pursue similar activities within their individual states. Moreover, the membership is eclectic in its activities and projects, ranging from black pastoral groups such as the Pastoral do Negro de Goiás to cultural and educational groups in Rio, São Paulo, Paraná and Sergipe. Groups from Rio de Janeiro and São Paulo tend to be better represented, although groups in many other regions play vital roles.[69]

CONEN's 'Letter from Minas Gerais' is open in its criticism of the government of Fernando Henrique Cardoso, which they believe has extended the neoliberal project initiated by President Collor in the early 1980s. To overcome racism, according to CONEN, implies 'guaranteeing equal and dignified conditions of life for all Brazilians and aiming to overcome not only racial, but class and gender biases as well'.[70]

The group '500 Anos de Resistência Negra, Indígena e Popular' is a national campaign, which brings together black, indigenous, popular and social justice groups to protest the country-wide celebrations planned to commemorate the arrival of the Portuguese explorer Pedro Alves Cabral to Brazil 500 years ago. Smaller groups, such as the lesser well-known Partido Popular Poder para a Maioria (PPPOMAR), inspired by rap groups with chapters in 15 different states, emerged in an attempt to affect the national elections of 1999, but had little influence. Still, the mere existence of the organization indicates a growing uneasiness and, in some cases rage, on the part of young Afro-Brazilians who no longer tolerate their exclusion from Brazilian society.[71]

NGOs

While NGOs face similar challenges, they are often able to obtain outside funding, and work beyond the confines of government parameters. A number of NGOs have emerged to make important contributions in the last decade. In general, there is little coordination among the various Afro-Brazilian organizations, in part due to lack of resources, but partly because of distinct aims and goals. There is even less coordination among groups from different states. Brazil's large landmass often makes communication and travel between cities in Brazil and cities in the United States or Great Britain easier than between cities in the south and the northeast of the interior. Black activists are often more aware of what is happening with the black community in the United States than events or issues in the interior, although this too is beginning to change, particularly since the proliferation of e-mail and access to the web.

NGOs tend to be of five major types: (1) those focusing on education and cultural promotion, (2) legal services which deal directly with civil and human rights issues and assist Afro-Brazilians in filing formal complaints with the authorities, (3) groups which deal with psychological needs such as self-esteem, (4) groups that focus on job-training and acquisition of skills for the market place, and (5) organizations which focus on the needs of Afro-Brazilian women. In many cases organizations carry out more than one of these tasks. Hundreds of organizations, some small with hardly any resources, others well-organized with strong traditions and permanent addresses, can be found throughout Brazil. It is impossible to list all of them so those presented are a range reflecting the struggles and gains of Afro-Brazilians.

The Centro de Estudos Afro-Asiáticos (Centre for Afro-Asiatic Studies), part of the Candido Mendes University in Rio, has been instrumental in compiling information and publishing materials on race in Brazil since 1973. Publications such as *Estudos Afro-Asiáticos* along with *Cadernos Negros*, and the historical texts published by Abdias do Nascimento leave a paper trail for researchers interested in Afro-Brazilians.

São Paulo has always been an important centre for activism. Among the many NGOs which have emerged to meet the growing demands within the black communities are a number of entities which focus on women and gender inequalities. Geledés Instituto da Mulher Negra, is perhaps the best known of them, providing educational, moral and legal services to the Afro-Brazilian community at large, but focusing on the plight of women in particular.[72] In Rio, the Instituto de Pesquisas da Cultura Negra (IPCN) has been a leader among Afro-Brazilian civil rights organizations since the 1970s, but others, such as the Centre for the Articulation of Marginalized Peoples (CEAP), have also played central roles. The Instituto Palmares de Direitos Humanos (Palmares Institute for Human Rights) is another important NGO in Rio which has several branches focusing on education and job skills. In the state of Minas Gerias, the Casa Dandara continues to serve the Afro-Brazilian community while the Coletivo de Empresários e Empreendedores Afro-Brasileiros de Triângulo Mineiro (CEABRA) which boasts over 60 members, caters to Afro-Brazilian businessmen and women.

The black population in the south is relatively small compared to that of other regions. The south has historically been sparsely populated, and received many European immigrants from Germany, Austria, Italy and, to a lesser extent, from Asia, relatively late in Brazilian history. Through the twentieth century, the Brazilian southern states have become demographically more white and less black. In Rio Grande do Sul, for example, the Afro-Brazilian population has diminished from 30 per cent in the mid-nineteenth century to 13 per cent today. In Santa Catarina Afro-Brazilians represent less than 10 per cent of the population.

Few studies have been conducted on the modern black populations of the south and many Brazilians seem surprised that there are any black people there at all. Afro-Brazilians have played crucial roles in the political and cultural life of the state, however. In 1998, the Catholic Church appointed a black bishop from Porto Alegre, Don Gílio, to serve as the Catholic spokesman responsible for opening a dialogue between the Catholic Church and African religions in Bahia. To many people's surprise, Alceu Collares became the first black governor of the state, serving his term from 1991 to 1994. Interestingly, it was Brazil's current president, Fernando Henrique Cardoso, who published one of the first modern sociological studies on black people in Rio Grande do Sul.[73]

Today a host of NGOs, education, and civil and human rights organizations, such as the MNU, the Forum de Articulação das Entidades Negras (Forum for the Articulation of Black Entities), Instituto Africa América (Iafra), Asociação das Mulheres Negras (Association of Black Women) exist along with the Assesoria do Negro (Black Advisory Service), a branch of the Office of the Coordinator of Human Rights and Citizenship of Porto Alegre. These are complemented by institutes such as the Núcleo de Estudos do Negro (Nucleus for the Study of Black People) in Florinopolis, the capital of Santa Catarina, and the Centro de Referencia do Material Didáctico Afro-Brasileira (Reference Centre for Afro-Brazilian Didactic Materials) of the Núcleo de Estudos Negros de Santa Catarina (NEN/SC), among others.[74]

Bahia is home to a number of groups at various stages of development. *Blocos afros*, or Afro-Brazilian carnival groups, such as Ilê Ayê and Olodum have well-known social programmes which mostly focus on education and consciousness-raising. Olodum's international reputation has enabled it to establish a number of extra-musical programmes, such as computer training for youngsters, in the historic district of the Pelourinho. According to Nelson Mendes, one of the directors of Olodum, these initiatives have been possible with help from other NGOs such as the Centre for the Democratization of Computer Science (DCI) in Rio, which donated a number of computers to the group. Ultimately Olodum would like to create a data bank of information on important Afro-Brazilians over the last 500 years.[75]

The Steven Biko Cooperative focuses more specifically on preparing poor Afro-Brazilians to take the university entrance examination (the *Vestibular*), but it has a broader goal of creating citizens who will participate in the political and social life of their communities. According to one ex-student, now a member of the board of coordinators, studying in the cooperative was not easy because the work is not only connected to personal issues of learning, but also to questions of self-esteem and political consciousness. Indeed, unlike ordinary preparation classes for the *Vestibular*, the first week at Steven Biko begins with a series of classes on human rights, legal rights and competences in the market place. According to the directorate, one of the major priorities is black consciousness: 'We want students with a certain quality, who understand the political role that a place in the university has. That student must understand that he or she is occupying a space which historically has been denied to black people.'[76]

Iyalodê: Centro de Referencia da Mulher Negra (Black Women's Reference Centre), a group of 13 female educators, has developed concrete programmes for female educators in state schools to help them deal with questions of race and gender. According to Iyalodê, working against racial and gender stereotypes in Bahia is particularly problematic since Bahia continues to be viewed as a racial paradise in the national imagination. Luiza Bairros, a member of the group, sees this myth as the major barrier to their educational work because denouncing racism remains something of a taboo, despite the fact that the racial inequalities, and the problems of women, are obvious.[77] Equally motivated is the recently formed Asantawaa, comprised of three women educators who aim to increase literacy among underprivileged black women, in addition to offering courses on citizenship.[78]

The programme 'A Cor da Bahia' (Colour of Bahia) at the Federal University of Bahia (UFBA), is a rare entity in Brazil. It sees itself as a direct descendant of the 'Class, Ethnicity and Social Movement Project' of UFBA which operated in the 1980s. The programme aims to research the position and contribution of black people in the workforce, in politics, education and culture. While the programme has conducted a number of fruitful activities within the Afro-Brazilian community, resources limit its work to the university itself. The programme offers small scholarships and support to undergraduate and graduate students, and encourages Afro-Brazilian students to pursue research in the field.

Groups like the Sociedade Afro-Sergipana de Estudos e Cidadania (SACI), which developed out of the União de Negros de Aracaju (UNA), aim to denounce racism in all of its forms and to inform Brazilians about their rights as well as to raise consciousness about race in general. Their publication, *Revista Gbàlà*, assists in this regard. Other groups such as Malungos-Organização Negra de Paraíba, Fórum das Entidades Negras do Maranhão (Forum of Black Entities of Maranhão, or FENMA) and the Fórum das Entidades do Ceará in Fortaleza (Forum of Entities of Ceará, or FENECE) share similar goals.

Djumbay in Recife, Pernambuco, has won respect from both the community at large and the state government. Created in 1992, Djumbay has divulged information about black cultural production through many community-wide events in its publication of the same name. The Pernambucan state government has recognized the importance of Djumbay's work, and has made it possible for more than 1,100 secondary schools and over 3,600 school teachers to receive copies of the newspaper, which researches and publishes stories about African culture and organization in Pernambuco, in Brazil and around the world. In addition, Djumbay's Núcleo de Identidade Racial (Racial Identity Nucleus, or NIR) offers legal and psychological help to victims of racism in conjunction with the State Secretary of Justice and the Ministry of Justice. Djumbay has managed to serve a diverse clientele of activists, government entities, and various cultural and religious groups.[79]

Art, music and black consciousness

Throughout history, Africans and their descendants have had a major impact on Brazil's rich and varied artistic and musical production. Afro-Brazilians have played a significant role in shaping Brazil's visual arts and many other art forms. Music has played a special role in the Afro-Brazilian community; indeed, to speak of Afro-Brazilian music seems unfair since Brazilian music is almost wholly African-inspired. That influence is seen in the many forms of *samba* and *pagode, afoxé* as well as in folk music in festivals such as *bumba meu boi* from the state of Maranhão to *partido alto* in Rio de Janeiro. Today certain musical forms are termed 'black music' (*funk, charme,* etc.) while others constitute a part of the eclectic 'popular Brazilian music', but that does not mean that the former has no European influences and that the latter is not based on African rhythms. These terms are merely a reflection of the consumer market. What is certain is that music has played a crucial role in African communities throughout the Americas.

For the descendants of African slaves in general, music provided one of the few opportunities for relaxation and escape after the day's work. But music also constitutes a vital part of a world view where feelings and desires are expressed through verse and accompanied by instruments. Musical composition, as oral tradition, also represents an important forum of communication, spreading information, stories and political consciousness.

In the years after abolition a number of Afro-Brazilian musicians (such as José Antonio da Silva Callado, Ernesto 'Donga' dos Santos and Alfredo da Rocha Vianna, popularly known as Pixinguinha), were acknowledged pioneers of Brazilian popular music. With the boom of the radio and recording industries in the 1930s, popular musicians had the power to reach millions of listeners. Thanks to the nationalist programmes of the Vargas era, Brazilian popular music was propagated with pride, and thus the work of many Afro-Brazilian musicians was showcased for the first time on a national level. Many of them were paid poorly or not at all, however, and until the late 1950s few black performers actually landed radio or record contracts for their own musical compositions. Furthermore, popular Afro-Brazilian cultural practices such as *capoeira*, an Afro-Brazilian martial arts form performed to the accompaniment of the *berimbau*, the *ganzá* and the tambourine, were often banned by the authorities.

In the 1930s, Carmen Miranda was voted the 'Queen of Samba' at a time when the music industry was dominated by men. She was one of the first women to become a nationally recognized popular musical entertainer. But the fact that she was white is not coincidental. Miranda often showcased the music of black performers when they could not get work. She brought many black people into the spotlight with her, including greats such as Sinval Silva the author of the classic 'Adeus Batucada' (and, incidentally, her chauffeur), and the Bahian composer Dorival Caymi whose songs inspired Miranda's own recreation of the Bahiana, the personality that would eventually take her to Hollywood.[80]

Many of the Brazilian musical compositions that deal with race or black characters are either stereotypical or racist, particularly prior to the 1960s. Famous compositions such as 'Teu cabelo não nega' (Your hair gives you away) and 'Nega de cabelo duro' (Hard-haired black woman) belittle Afro-Brazilian women, while 'Nego no samba' paints a stereotypical picture of dancing black people.

It is undeniable that Afro-Brazilians have always taken part in Brazilian celebrations, particularly carnival, but in places like Rio de Janeiro and Salvador few Afro-Brazilians control the images projected of black people, and even fewer reap direct economic profits from these celebrations.

In her study of carnival groups in Rio de Janeiro in the 1980s, Alison Raphael has shown that Rio's carnival has become a micro-enterprise with few Afro-Brazilian owners.[81] Indeed, the prices for seats in the famous *sambódromo*, where *the escolas de samba* parade, are exorbitant, and the huge profits from ticket sales rarely reach the *favelas* from which the majority of the participants come. In Salvador, carnival may seem more democratic and less expensive, but it is not without its racial problems. The Bahian equivalent to Rio's *escolas de samba* are the *trío eléctricos*, groups that ride atop a car or float, but they are much less formal and do not necessarily play one particular style of music. The cost of participating in the trío is quite high and few black people have traditionally paraded with many of them. This constitutes de facto segregation in a city known as a major centre of African culture in the Americas. In the 1970s, two Bahian *blocos afros* burst on the scene to change that: Ilê Ayê and Olodum.

Created in 1974 in Liberdade, the poor suburb of Salvador and the centre of black consciousness, Ilê Ayê was the first Afro-Bahian carnival group to celebrate blackness through its music, lyrics and aesthetics. According to Vovô, secretary of the group, Ilê Ayê, which means 'Black World' was influenced by the emergence of black pride in the United States, but in Salvador, a city with a majority of Afro-Brazilians, its ideology was and still is marked by controversy.[82] Ilê Ayê's membership is restricted to black people since it celebrates black beauty, black hair and develops rhythms that combine samba with religious drumming from *Candomblé* religious ceremonies. All of the group's musical numbers are rigorously researched and attempt to educate listeners about the 'Black World' as well as entertain them. Indeed, many black activists in Salvador admit with pride that through Ilê Ayê's musical compositions they began to learn about important Afro-Brazilian historical events and heroes such as Zumbí dos Palmares and the Revolt of Buzios.[83]

That Ilê Ayê's presence sparks controversy illustrates the unique racist nature of Salvador society. The politics of Ilê Ayê has always been clear. Its organizers wanted to create a black world for the cultivation and celebration of blackness, and avoid commercialization and cooption by white people. But this was also a protest against the mainstream Bahian carnival groups which included few black people. In one of its signature songs, Ilê Ayê warns: 'Wake up to see the Black World/ The song of the African race/ fluent/ Bahian/ Babá Oke/ Oxalá and Xangô protect you/ the Black World.'[84] Ironically this affirmation was branded racist by Bahians who decried the fact that white people were not allowed into the group.

On the heels of Ilê Ayê, a host of other black groups emerged in neighbourhoods in Salvador and around the country. Today Bahian groups such as Ara Ketu, Muzenza, Malê Debalê and Olodum are household names, and serve important social as well as musical functions. Olodum, a *samba-reggae* group, has had particular success in linking black consciousness with a broad appeal through marketing campaigns. Olodum's drumming director, Neguinho da Samba, once a member of Ilê Ayê, has been responsible for much of the group's musical discipline. For some black activists Olodum's commercial success has come with a price, but lenders like Nelson Mendes defend the group's decision to reach out to the wider community and to allow non-black people access to the group, insisting that Olodum has been able to export Afro-Bahian pride through association with artists such as Paul Simon, and in turn has been able to offer much more to the community than it would have been able to otherwise.[85]

Outside Bahia, nationally known groups such as Cidade Negra (Black City), whose lead singer Toni Garrido starred in the 1999 Brazilian remake of the 1959 classic *Orfeu Negro* (entitled simply *Orfeu*), have helped create a Brazilian reggae movement which celebrates racial solidarity. Musical influences from the Caribbean and the United States have inspired a number of Brazilian musical groups who play their own brands of rap, hip hop and Afro-reggae. Afro-Brazilian activists continue to see black North American music and politically conscious music in Brazil as an important point of reference for the black movement in Brazil.[86] The 1990s, saw the emergence of female and male hip hop artists and rappers, such as the Damas do Rap (Ladies of Rap) from Rio, PMC e Líder Boy (from Minas Gerais) and Thaíde and D.J. Hum, considered by many the founders of the hip hop movement in São Paulo.

The lyrics of 'Negro com attitude' (Black with an attitude) are typical of the political message of many rap and hip hop groups who many credit with raising racial consciousness and promoting black pride among Afro-Brazilian youth: 'If you're born black and poor you're screwed/ The racist society does everything to put an end to you/… Black people where is your attitude? Black people show your attitude/ Black people: live with attitude and then we can change things.'[87]

According to some activists, other pop groups such as Negritude Junior have had a positive impact on many black youth since they sing about black beauty and their members serve as positive role models, essential elements in the education and promotion of black pride. On another level, veteran singers Caetano Veloso and Gilberto Gil, both Bahian and founders of the *tropicalia* movement of the late 1960s, and two of the most critically acclaimed Brazilian composers and entertainers, have always understood the power of music as a political force, and both have frequently exposed Brazilian racial inequality. In their 1996 recording 'Haiti', Gil and Veloso excavated and criticized Brazilian racial hierarchy, using the beating (and murder) of prisoners in São Paulo to record a song of protest:

> *'111 defenseless prisoners, but black,*
> *they are all black,*
> *or almost black, or almost white*
> *almost black because they are so poor,*
> *and the poor are like garbage and everyone*
> *knows how to treat black people.'*[88]

In the face of such conditions, political consciousness and education becomes not only a programme of survival but a critical call for change.

Afro-Brazilians: contemporary demographics

As a community Afro-Brazilians are still economically marginalized and politically disenfranchised, and are at the bottom in relation to all social and economic indicators. Some governmental as well as non-governmental organizations (NGOs) and private institutions have now begun to gather statistics on race and ethnicity, although past negligence makes historical comparisons difficult. Statistics on Afro-Brazilians remain intrinsically problematic because of poor data-gathering practices, and the myriad of terms that Brazilians continue to use to define themselves from region to region.

In general, it is safe to conclude that the Afro-Brazilian population has always been underestimated so most demographic figures can be taken as a minimum. But this statement needs further clarification. Afro-Brazilians are drastically under-counted if by Afro-Brazilians we mean all Brazilians with some African ancestry, since that would include a majority of Brazilians. As President Fernando Henrique Cardoso declared publicly, 'Eu tambem tenho um pé na cozinha' ('I also have one foot in the kitchen' – an expression used to refer to people with African ancestry since traditionally black people were responsible for running the kitchens, and because much Brazilian cooking is African-derived). If we mean by Afro-Brazilians those who have visible African features (however problematic and essentialist a deduction), then they are hopelessly under-counted in national data. In general, however, the term 'Afro-Brazilian' refers to *pretos* and *afro-mestiços*, bearing in mind that many *afro-mestiços* consider themselves white. Others, such as the mayor of São Paulo, Celso Pitta, insist on being called black. Many activists, such as Carlos Alberto Medeiros, sub-secretary of the Secretariat for Human Rights and Citizenship in Rio de Janeiro, understandably express frustration when public officials refuse to accept their *negritude*, or blackness. Medeiros was delighted that President Cardoso stated that he believed in principle in policies of affirmative action. The promotion of General Jorge Alves de Cavalho was an important appointment for the black community, but Medeiros expressed dismay when he read that Cavalho had said that his colour was 'olive'.[89]

In the 1990 census report the Brazilian Institute for Geography and Statistics (IBGE) used five basic categories for colour or race: White (Branco), Black (Preto),

Yellow (Amarela), Indigenous (Indígena) and *Parda*. *Parda* translates literally as brown, but is, by and large, synonymous with *afro-mestiço*, although it may contain some *indio-mestiços* with no African roots. Those who did not respond positively to any of the above categories were placed under the category 'Not Declared'. The racial breakdown of a total population of 146,815,796 inhabitants was as follows: 75,704,927 White; 7,335,136 Black; 62,316,064 *Parda*; 630,656 Yellow; 294,135 Indigenous; and 534,878 Not Declared.

According to these statistics, a majority of Brazilians are white. *Pretos* represent approximately 5 per cent of the population. If the approximately 42 per cent *Parda* category represents a combination of *mulatos*, brown-skinned people and *cafusos* (as all calculations will assume), then Afro-Brazilians represent a total of 47 per cent of the population. Even if the number of *indio-mestiços* with no African roots is as much as 10 per cent of *pardos*, for example, given that black people are over-represented in poor areas which continue to be under-represented in census reports, it is possible to use the 47 per cent figure as a plausible and credible minimum.[90]

Brazil is divided into five major regions: the North (the states of Rondonia, Acre, Amazonas, Roraima, Pará, Amapá and Tocantins); the Northeast (Maranhão, Piaui, Ceará, Rio Grande do Norte, Paraiba, Pernambuco, Alagoas, Sergipe, Bahia); the Southeast (Minas Gerais, Espirito Santo, Rio de Janeiro and São Paulo); the South (Paraná, Santa Catarina, Rio Grande do Sul); and the Central-West (Mato Grosso do Sul, Mato Grosso, Goias and Brasilia, the Federal District). Although Brazil's geographical territory is immense, according to the 1990 census report almost 76 per cent of the population lives in urban centres: or, more specifically, 81 per cent of white people, 74 per cent of *pretos* and 69 per cent of *pardos*. These percentages differ considerably from the indigenous population, 76 per cent of whom live in non-urban areas.[91]

Afro-Brazilians can be found in every region of Brazil. Historically Africans and their descendants played crucial roles in every region even though in some regions today they are less visible. The two most populous regions are the Southeast and the Northeast, and the majority of Afro-Brazilians can be found in these two regions. According to the 1990 census 1,303,625 (17.8 per cent) of *pretos* live in the state of Rio de Janeiro; a further 1,199,982 (16.4 per cent) live in the state of Bahia, followed by 1,153,982 (15.7 per cent) in São Paulo and 1,057,381 (14 per cent) in Minas Gerais. *Pardos* are most numerous in the state of Bahia (8,190,285 or 13 per cent); followed by São Paulo (6,871,613 or 11 per cent), Minas Gerais (6,541,876 or 10.5 per cent) and Pernambuco (4,517,317, 7.2 per cent).[92]

Bahia, which is often referred to as the African Mecca in the New World, has the largest Afro-Brazilian population of 9,390,267 *pretos* and *pardos*, 79 per cent of the total population of the state, compared to 78 per cent of the population in Maranhão (another state in the northeast of Brazil), 44 per cent of the state of Rio de Janeiro and 25 per cent of the population of São Paulo, the largest state in the nation.

The representation of Afro-Brazilians in national culture

For much of Brazil's history Afro-Brazilians are absent from most official images. After independence, the symbol of Brazil was the monarchy even though Afro-Brazilians, many of them slaves, constituted the majority of the population. Until the 1930s, Brazil promoted a white image of the country which was replaced by a white celebration of racial mixing and racial democracy.

The military dictatorship (from 1964 to the early 1980s) meant that little attention was given to social problems or race relations for almost twenty years. Moreover the sense of racial democracy and unity continued to be pushed as the famous slogan of the era: 'Brazil, Love it or Leave it!' attests. The social and cultural changes that emerged in the 1960s in Europe and the United States did have an impact on Brazil, but largely in the area of culture. The Black Power movement, Malcom X and Martin Luther King had an important influence on Brazilians, although Afro-Brazilians' ability to translate the new consciousness which emerged in the United States to Brazil was limited by the dictatorship. The social justice platforms of most underground resistance groups, leftists and human rights activists contained a list of human rights abuses, including torture, forced exile and censorship. Racial intolerance constituted another example, but it was hardly at the top of the list, despite the fact that, as Abdias do Nascimento has pointed out, Africans and Afro-Brazilians had been tortured, censored and exiled for centuries.

Researchers such as Florestan Fernandes and Octávio Ianni were pioneers in exposing Brazilian racial problems, and important works such as Anani Dzidzienyo's report on Afro-Brazilians in 1979 provided much-needed information for Brazilians in exile.[93] (The report was difficult to obtain in Brazil, although it was not necessarily officially censored.) Civil rights activist and former senator Abdias do Nascimento recalls that he had little empirical information on racial themes in Brazil, and that Dzidzienyo's report was one of the few with which he became familiar while teaching in the United States in the 1970s.[94]

One of the few forums where African themes were treated nationally was Brazil's cinema. *Cinema novo*, a politically orientated cinema of the 1960s, provided some of the first images of Afro-Brazilian customs, poverty and lifestyles, particularly from non-urban areas. Film-makers such as Nelson Pereira dos Santos and Glauber Rocha made *cinema novo* a cinema of the oppressed and aimed to expose Brazil's underdevelopment. However, many of the images were one-dimensional, reinforcing stereotypes, since few 'ordinary' or urban Afro-Brazilians appeared on the screen. Beginning in the 1970s, Carlos (Cacá) Diegues began creating some of Brazil's most memorable Afro-Brazilian film images while providing important opportunities for black actors and actresses. But many of Diegues' images, such as those presented in the classic *Xica da Silva* (1976), downplay racial violence or problems.

Xica da Silva was an important black woman in Brazilian history, and her story underscores the difficult position of African women in Brazilian colonial society as well as demonstrating that victims of slavery also used the system to seek personal advantage. Xica, like with thousands of black women in the Americas, gained favours from her master, who found her sexually appealing. Although Diegues' film *Xica da Silva*, inspired by a samba school's carnival parade, was immensely popular in Brazil, this particular treatment underplays the difficult position of African slaves, and violence against women in general. The tendency to downplay racial conflict and ethnic violence and to highlight inter-racial sexual relations and miscegenation in films like *Xica da Silva* and *Carlota Joaquina* (1995) was not just typical under the military dictatorship (1964–79), but represents a pattern common to both the Brazilian cinema and television.[95]

The political opening of the late 1970s and early 1980s allowed for the emergence of a contemporary black protest movement. Despite such movements, unfavourable stereotypes of black people remain prevalent in Brazil's media. Were it not for these stereotypical representations, however, there would be even fewer Afro-Brazilian images in the media today.

In many respects little has changed since Dzidzienyo's 1979 Minority Rights' report.[96] Legally Brazilians are protected by many more civil rights, and there are signs of a growing Afro-Brazilian middle class, particularly in the arts, music and in sports, but in universities and in top or middle echelons of political and economic institutions black people are still grossly under-represented. Visitors to Brazil tend not perceive these inequalities since, in public spaces, people of different social classes and races intermingle with ease. Still, colonial stereotypes of black people continue to exist, and Brazilian society tends to dismiss many Afro-Brazilian success stories as exceptions to the rule. Stereotypes are used as yardsticks to encourage individuals to live down to pre-imposed static images of groups. Gilberto Gil's poignant song 'A mão de limpeza' (The hand that cleans) clearly denotes this very predicament.

Afro-Brazilian women are stereotyped as promiscuous or erotic and are associated with certain professions like as the *mulatas* of carnival and nightclub dancers the world over. These images mask the power and gender relations which aim 'to keep black people in their place'. Souvenirs, statues and t-shirts depicting naked black women, which are sold in almost every corner store in the Pelourinho in

FURTHER PUBLICATIONS AVAILABLE FROM MRG.

AFRO-CENTRAL AMERICANS: REDISCOVERING THE AFRICAN HERITIGE

Central Americans of African ancestry have historically been an oppressed and neglected minority. Almost all descended from slaves, and representing a sizeable proportion of the population in many countries of the region, they have generally been denied access to power, influence or material progress. MRG's Report seeks to challenge the 'invisibility' of people of African descent to wider Central American society. Focusing on Mexico, Nicaragua, Panama, Costa Rica, Belize and Honduras, the Report highlights Afro-Central Americans' significant contribution to the region, often in the face of marginalization and racism.
1996. ISBN 1 897693 51 6. 36pp. £4.95/US$8.95 plus P&P

THE MAYA OF GUATEMALA

More than 500 years after the arrival of Europeans in the Americas, the Maya, descendants of one of the greatest pre-Columbian civilizations, not only exist but are thriving. The survival of 21 different Maya speaking peoples in Guatemala is a living testimony to their powers of resistance. In recent years, the brutal conquest of their cities and mountain lands by Spanish conquistadors in the early sixteenth century, has been replayed in all its horrors. In the 1980s alone, the Guatemalan army is conservatively estimated to have murdered 20,000 Maya. Whole villages were wiped out, as at least 120,000 fled into Mexico and 500,000 became internal refugees.
1994, reprint with Udpate 1997. ISBN 1 897693 55 9. 50pp (plus 4pp insert). £4.95/US$8.95 plus P&P

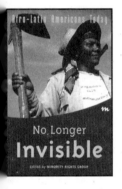

NO LONGER INVISIBLE: AFRO-LATIN AMERICANS TODAY

Numbering perhaps 125 million people, Latin Americans of African ancestry have generally been denied access to power, influence or material progress. While Afro-Latin Americans have frequently challenged their oppression with some success, and have seen many aspects of their culture absorbed into mainstream Latin American life, persistent myths of 'colour-blind racial democracy' and *blanqueamiento* ('whitening') mask the insidious and often brutal reality of the discrimination they face. This book charts the Afro-Latin American experience from slavery to contemporary times, showing the contrasts as well as the similarities across the region.
1995. ISBN 1 873194 85 4. (paperback) 432pp. £12.95/US$24.95 plus P&P and 1995. ISBN 1 873194 80 3. (hardback) 432pp. £29.95/US$49.95 plus P&P

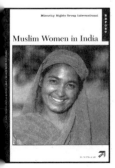

NEW REPORT
MUSLIM WOMEN IN INDIA

Opportunities for Muslim women in India to raise their concerns over access to education rights and work opportunities, or to raise issues within Muslim personal law – including marriage, divorce and personal freedoms – are often severely restricted. MRG's Report discusses both the historical and contemporary position of Muslim women in India and within their own communities and their involvement in the wider women's movements. The author further discusses the effects of the rise of the Hindu right-wing on Muslim women's rights and freedoms.
1999. ISBN 1897693 47 8. 40pp. £5.95/US$10.95 plus P&P

MINORITIES IN SOUTHEAST EUROPE: INCLUSION AND EXCLUSION

Ethnic conflict in Southeast Europe has led to recent wars in this region and the associated tragedies of 'ethnic cleansing' and mass migration. MRG's timely new Report examines the key issues influencing minority/majority relations and provides an historical framework for understanding the roles of ethnicity and religion in the formation of political systems. The Report discusses issues of self-determination and territorial autonomy, and provides a valuable insight into the major factors that provoke inter-group conflict.
1998. ISBN 1 897693 42 7. 40pp. £4.95/US$8.95 plus P&P

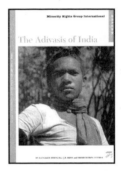

NEW REPORT
THE ADIVASIS OF INDIA

The Adivasis are indigenous peoples with distinct languages, religions and forms of self-government who maintain deep bonds to their land and respect for nature. However, India has ignored their demands for recognition and taken steps which threaten their very survival. The Report highlight the forcible displacement of Adivasis from their territories to make way for industrialization; coal, forest and mineral exploitation; for tourism and wildlife parks. Focusing on three specific regions: Jharkhand, the Blue Mountains and the North-East it calls for an end to discrimination, and for the recognition of Adivasis' rights.
1999. ISBN 1 897693 32 X. 40pp. £5.95/US$10.95 plus P&P

NEW REPORT
FORESTS AND INDIGENOUS PEOPLES OF ASIA

For indigenous peoples in Asia, forests have traditionally represented their lands and their livelihoods. Yet in recent years the region has lost more than half of its forests, threatening the survival of forest-dwellers due to economic and cultural impoverishment, human rights abuses, land loss and integration into the global marketplace. This Report focuses on five states – Bangladesh, India, Malaysia, Nepal and Thailand – describing how logging, hydropower schemes, commercial plantations and settlers are displacing more and more indigenous peoples, as well as how these peoples are mobilizing against this environmental destruction and the loss of their lands and livelihoods.
1999. ISBN 1 897693 77 X. 32pp. £5.95/US$10.95 plus P&P

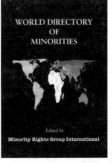

WORLD DIRECTORY OF MINORITIES

An authoritative reference book on the history and contemporary situation of ethnic, linguistic an religious minorities worldwide, covering more than 200 states and dependent territories and over 700 minority groups. Organized by region and country, this study offers a pertinent analysis of international, regional and local minority rights issues, and indicates major areas of intercommunity tension.
1997. ISBN 1 873194 36 6. Hardback only. 856pp. £100.00/US$145 plus P&P. Please contact MRG for details of discounts now available on this title.

To order any of these titles or a free copy of our full Publications Catalogue - see overleaf

ORDER FORM

QUANTITY	TITLE/ITEM	PRICE	TOTAL

* 1–5 items: add 15% of sub total UK; 20% of sub total overseas surface; 25% of sub total airmail. 6+ items: add 10% of sub total UK; 15% of sub total overseas surface; 25% of sub total airmail. Subscription prices are inclusive of postage.

Sub total

Postage*

Total due

I would like to pay by cheque / visa / mastercard / bank transfer *(delete as appropriate)*

- **Cheques** should be made payable to Minority Rights Group in UK sterling or US dollars and drawn on a UK or US bank.
- **Direct transfers** to National Westminster Bank, Villiers House, 38 Strand, London WC2N 5JB, UK. Account sort code: 60 40 05 Account nos: 01409182 (UK sterling); 02860732 (US dollars). Please send a remittance advice note to the Sales Department, MRG, London.
- **Visa/mastercard** (include card name and address if different from below)

Expiry date

Please deliver goods to: Name . . . .

Address . . . .

. . . .

. . . . Post code . . . .

Return form to: Minority Rights Group International, 379 Brixton Road, London SW9 7DE, UK.

Fax +44 (0)171 738 6265. Telephone/email orders accepted: +44 (0)20 7978 9498; minority.rights@mrgmail.org

ORDERING INFORMATION

MRG publications are available from all good bookshops or direct from MRG, UK.

SUBSCRIPTIONS

The easiest way to obtain all new titles is to become an annual subscriber. You will receive 6 new Reports and Profiles (4pp summaries of Reports), 2 issues of MRG's newsletter *Outsider* and MRG's Annual Report. Rates: Individual (inc 2nd class/surface mail) £30/US$48; Individual (inc air mail) £45/US$70; Institution (inc 2nd class/surface mail) £45/US$72; Institution (inc air mail) £60/US$97. To order your subscription use the form above.

TRADE REPRESENTATION

UK & Ireland (all publications)
Central Books, 99 Wallis Road, London E9 5LN, UK,
Tel +44 (0)20 8986 4854, Fax +44 (0)20 8533 5821. Email: orders@centbks.demon.co.uk

Denmark, Finland, Iceland, Norway, Sweden, (all publications)
D Richard Bowen, PO Box 30037, S-200 61, Malmö 30, Sweden.
Tel +46 40 16 12 00, fax +46 40 16 12 08.

North America (books only)
Paul & Company Publishers Consortium Inc, PO Box 442, Concord, MA 01742, USA.
Tel +1 978 369 3049, fax +1 978 369 2385.

INSPECTION/EXAMINATION COPIES

For further information contact the Marketing Department at MRG.

**For more information and a full catalogue: tel +44 (0)171 978 9498, fax +44 (0)171 738 6265
email minority.rights@mrgmail.org or visit www.minorityrights.org**

MRG: TELL US WHAT YOU THINK

At MRG we are reviewing our publication formats and content, and we need your feedback. We will use the information to evaluate this Report and to review how material is presented. **Please spend a few minutes completing this form, then fold and return to us. As a thank you for your reply we will send you a free copy of *MRG's Report on Afro-Central Americans: Rediscovering the African Heritage*.**

1. Please tell us how you obtained this Report:

☐ MRG annual subscription
☐ Purchased direct from MRG
☐ Purchased from a stall at a conference or event
☐ Purchased from a bookshop or commercial outlet
☐ Complimentary copy
☐ Don't know
☐ Other - please specify:

....

2. What are the main ways in which you will use this Report (e.g. academic/research interest, campaigning/activist, general knowledge)?:

....
....
....
....

3. If you received this publication through your work, please tell us what type of organization you work for: (e.g. NGO, Government Department, University etc):

....

4. How useful do you think this Report will be to you/your organization?:

☐ Very Useful   ☐ Useful   ☐ Not Useful

5. Are there ways that the Report could have been made more useful?:

....
....
....

6. Do you have any other comments on the quality, accuracy or topicality of MRG Reports?:

....
....
....
....

7. Please tell us which parts of the Report you find most useful by numbering these options 1-6 and indicate which sections you did not read (*1 for most useful and 6 for least useful*):

☐ Preface   ☐ Did not read
☐ Profile   ☐ Did not read
☐ Main text   ☐ Did not read
☐ Maps, tables/graphics   ☐ Did not read
☐ Bibliography   ☐ Did not read
☐ Recommendations   ☐ Did not read
☐ Other, please specify:

....

8. MRG is considering changing the format of its publications. Please tell us which format you would prefer by numbering these options 1- 5 (*1 for your preferred format, 5 for your least preferred format*):

☐ Report format (A4 thin) as present
☐ Book format (A5 thicker)
☐ Available on the Internet
    (for which a charge may be made)
☐ No preference
☐ Other: please specify:

....

9. Do you have any comments on the presentation of MRG Reports (e.g. are they easy to read, would you prefer something photocopied or something which looked more glossy)?:

....

MRG will not give your details to other organizations but we may have other publications which are of interest to you. If you would like more information about other publications/events, please put your details in the box below and specify your areas of interest:

Areas of interest:..
....

☐ *If you don't want to receive details of other MRG publications/events, please tick here*

Your details (optional):

Name:..
Organization:..
....
Address:..
....
....
Country: ....
Telephone: ....
Fax: ....
Email address: ....

We would welcome further comments on any aspect of our publications or other work, please continue overleaf if you would like to expand on any of the above or raise areas not covered by our questions.

You can also fax this form to us or send it directly from our website at www.minorityrights.org

Minority Rights Group International
379 Brixton Road, London, SW9 7DE, UK.
Tel: +44 (0)20 7978 9498
Fax: +44 (0)20 7738 6265
Email: minority.rights@mrgmail.org

Additional space for further comments:

←—— fold and glue to this edge ——→

Return to:

Minority Rights Group International
379 Brixton Road
London
SW9 7DE   UK

Salvador, Bahia, are not celebrating Afro-Brazilian sexuality that has survived Portuguese colonization and western bourgeois mores, but rather are exploiting blackness in general, and black women in particular, in a capitalist market where racial differences can be exoticized, commodified and sold. The Afro-Brazilian poetess Elisa Lucinda criticizes the Brazilian commodification of Afro-Brazilian women in her poignant 'Mulata exportação' (*Mulata* exportation), reminding her readers that inter-racial sexual relations have not diminished racism in Brazil:

> *'What a beautiful black woman…/*
> *Come be my excuse.../*
> *Come be my folklore/*
> *Come and be my thesis…/*
> *I remember the slave quarters/*
> *and you the Master's house*
> *And together we are going to truthfully write another history?…*
> *Because having sex with a mulatta does not mean that you've stopped being a racist!'*

Black women in Brazil face great challenges relative to other population groups. In addition to lower earning power, regardless of education, Afro-Brazilian women face higher incidence of health problems such as breast cancer and have more hysterectomies (15.9 per cent) than white women (3.6 per cent).[97] Many black women activists note that Brazilian men, both white and black, are socialized to think as the old racist saying goes that 'white women are for marriage, *mulatas* for sex, and black women for work'. While there is no data corroborating this tendency in Brazil, the fact that a number of highly visible successful black men have chosen blonde women as their partners has met with a critical response. It is possible that black men may be avoiding association with other black people in another attempt to deny their blackness, and suggesting this may provide an opportunity for black people to reflect on their choices. On the other hand, this criticism remains problematic since it does not encourage reconciliation among black women and men based on choices they have made. Moreover, it suggests that individuals ought to marry or choose partners simply because of their race, which is itself both essentialist and problematic (how dark?, what hair texture?, eye colour?) and does not take into consideration a host of other factors that affect human relations.[98]

Undoubtedly, the official standard for beauty around the world, which seemingly privileges 'white characteristics', operates in Brazil as well. Personal choices are complex and difficult to analyse without knowledge of motivations, but the choices of the media are quite another matter. Positive Afro-Brazilian images in the media are rare, and throughout this century Brazilians have been uncomfortable with black people representing them abroad. This is only now beginning to change. In terms of beauty, Brazilians have had a 'black' Miss Brazil, the *gaucha* Deise Nunes de Souza in 1986. It was painfully obvious, however, that Miss de Souza had never been referred to or considered herself *negra* before she was crowned Miss Brazil. Thus, the rule of 'whitening', in an age of multiculturalism was conveniently inverted to

reflect a 'darkening', which could be used as an example of Brazil's lack of racial prejudice. But, as Dzidzienyo reported in 1979, inter-racial marriages are not as common as one might think in Brazil.[99] Furthermore, inter-racial couples are as unlikely to be seen on television and in the news as Afro-Brazilian images in general.[100]

It is unclear whether racial prejudice against black people exists on the same scale among gays and lesbians as among heterosexuals. Grassroots movements across Brazil often work in cooperation with Afro-Brazilian groups. Gay and lesbian organizations are not racially homogeneous forums but multi-ethnic organizations within which Afro-Brazilians and white people have worked together for a long time.

It is noteworthy that in Afro-Brazilian religions which celebrate human nature, homosexuals are welcome. In 1998 Luis Motta and Marcelo Cerqueira, gay activists in Salvador, Bahia, published a book, *As Religióes Afro-Brasileiras Na Luta Contra a AIDS* (Afro-Brazilian religions and the fight against AIDS), which reported that the large number of homosexuals combined with some of the religious practices (letting blood, piercing, etc.) led to a high incidence of AIDS among worshippers. Joint efforts with gay groups have led to a raised awareness of the disease and a change of practice in places of worship. But these positive steps are rarely reported in the national media.

Still anyone living in Brazil in the 1990s will notice that there are more Afro-Brazilian actors and actresses on television and the silver screen today than a decade ago. More often than not, though, Afro-Brazilians are more likely to be found in stereotypical roles as maids or servants, or in historical dramas or *novelas* about slavery or the colonial era, or occasionally as dancers musicians or comedians. The popular children's TV programme directed by Xuxa, the blonde host, who dances, sings and plays games with groups of Brazilian kids, is typical since Afro-Brazilian children are absent.

Several vintage actors such as Milton Gonçalves and Antônio Pitanga follow in the tradition of the great Afro-Brazilian actor Grande Othelo, who as a comic was able to break into many forums previously unknown to black actors. TEN provided opportunities to numerous actors and actresses who continue to play important roles in television and film, among them Haroldo Costa, Lea Garcia and Ruth de Souza who are joined by others such as Zéze Motta, the star *of Xica da Silva*. Among the many television presenters and reporters in Brazil, Afro-Brazilians are also visibly absent, although the presence of Glória María Mattos da Silva (of TV Globo) is one notable exception. Brazilians working in television, magazines and other print media often argue that no one will pay to see black people on the screen, or pay black people to market their products, but this seems more like a rationalization than reality

Recent stories of Afro-Brazilians in Brazil's mainstream press indicate that 'mainstream' is synonymous with white, and that Brazilians are not sure how to cover Afro-Brazilian public figures. Often references to their colour or race overshadow their important contributions to society. In February 1997, the Afro-Brazilian mayor of São Paulo appeared on the cover of the well-respected São Paulo based magazine, *República* with the title 'O homen sem cor: de como Celso Pitta inventa a própria raça para governar os brancos' (A man without colour: how Celso Pitta invented his own race to govern whites). In March 1998 the same magazine featured the artist Emanoel Araújo, current director of the Pinacoteca de São Paulo, above the title 'A cor de Emanoel Araújo' (The colour of Emanoel Araújo). In June 1998, *Veja* magazine's cover story 'De preconceito ao sucesso' (From prejudice to success) featured a number of well-known Afro-Brazilians to illustrate how successful black people – all of them either entertainers or football players – had fought racism. Thus, the Brazilian public rarely sees the rich diversity within the Afro-Brazilian community.

Within the last five years a number of Afro-Brazilian magazines have emerged depicting Afro-Brazilians and catering to a growing demand for news about black people in Brazil and around the world from a black perspective. *Raça Brasil*, and *Black People* are two of the best-known examples. *Raça Brasil*, which resembles a Brazilian version of the American magazines *Ebony* or *Essence*, has been particularly successful, although many in the black movement criticize its superficial images and its focus on consumerism. This criticism is not unfounded, yet it misses the importance of a magazine which simply says to Brazilians: 'We are here!' To be sure the Afro-Brazilian press has a long tradition going back to the nineteenth century, yet *Raça Brasil* is the first Afro-Brazilian magazine since *abertura* to enjoy national commercial success.

In 1999 *Raça Brasil* has begun to balance its desire to sell magazines to a popular market with its concern for social and political rights through a number of columns which showcase cases of discrimination, and ways in which Afro-Brazilians have successfully combated them, highlighting activist groups which provide important services to the Afro-Brazilian community and give psychological advice to Afro-Brazilian communities. Of these new areas, the last is most problematic since it features a short pop-psychology question-and-answer section which invariably focuses on the issue of low self-esteem. The magazine focuses too often on this issue, assuming that this is a major problem for Afro-Brazilians, rather than calling for political, social and cultural participation as citizens. On the other hand, a purely political magazine would not have such broad appeal. Furthermore it would run the risk of being called 'racist' in Brazil.

Afro-Brazilians in politics

It is indisputable that Afro-Brazilians have made significant inroads in the political arena since the 1980s, but their numbers are still out of step with demographic trends. As one black activist explained it, 'White people don't vote for black people, and most black people don't vote for black people.'[101] While this may be true, it is not so much that black people do not vote for other black people because they are black, but a reflection of the tenuous relationship between political parties in Brazil and the various components of a diverse black movement. Few black political leaders run campaigns with racialized agendas, but Afro-Brazilian candidates can be found seeking office at national, state and local level.

Since the early 1980s many political parties have chosen black candidates to represent them in local elections, but few are elected.

Brazil's political legislature is similar to that of the United States. The republic is governed by three distinct political institutions: the federal government which has absolute sovereignty in the international arena; the 26 states (and the Federal District), each with its own state government with autonomy within the state's boundaries; and the municipalities, which are discrete divisions within individual states. Brazil's National Congress, the body responsible for formulating national laws, is comprised of two separate bodies: the House of Deputies, or the Congress, and the Federal Senate. Three senators from each state of the union comprise the Federal Senate while the House of Deputies is comprised of a given number of deputies, depending on the population of the state, and ranging from 8 to 70 (today there are a total of 505). Each state has its own legislative assembly made up of state deputies or congressmen and women. Municipalities, formed according to the size of the state, are governed by the Town Council or Assembly made up of a number of aldermen and women (or assemblymen/women).

The percentage of Afro-Brazilians in the federal branches of government (the Senate and the House) has traditionally been small, but so is the number of Afro-Brazilians elected to the state legislatures. In 1987, Benedita da Silva from the state of Rio de Janeiro became the first black women ever to be elected to Congress. She represents hope for the future in her defence of black and poor people in Brazil. She has strong religious convictions and is supported by religious groups, but she is not dogmatic. She has worked with other groups that are discriminated against in the state of Rio, including homosexuals who supported her in the last election. In Rio, da Silva's party, the PT, has fielded a number of Afro-Brazilian candidates over the past decade, and many of them have won state and municipal elections, among them Marcelo Dias (state congressman – PT) and Jurema Batista (City Councilwoman – PT/RJ). Both the PT and the PDT have created important groups within their parties to discuss issues of race, although the PDT's 'National Secretariat to Combat Racism' plays a more institutional role.

Afro-Brazilians can be elected to public office in many areas of Brazil. Celso Pitta's past election as mayor of the city of São Paulo should not go unnoticed since Afro-Brazilians are not a majority there. Moreover, white politicians such as Paulo Maluf in São Paulo, Leonel Brizola in Rio de Janeiro as well as Fernando Henrique Cardoso realize the political importance of supporting black candidates. While many view this support as opportunistic, the fact is that it is still unprecedented, and Brazil is beginning to see more Afro-Brazilians in high political positions than ever before. President Cardoso's appointment of Pelé, the first black cabinet member, to the Ministry of Sports, was one example. The Ministry of Sports was later accused of improper use of government funds and eventually abolished in a cloud of controversy. Afro-Brazilian politicians are no more corrupt than white politicians, however, though the way that the media and society at large judges them may give this impression. Stereotypes play an important role in keeping Afro-Brazilians out of office, but they can be overcome.

The 1992 municipal elections in Salvador, the capital of Bahia, long considered the centre of African culture in Brazil provides several important insights into the role of race at the municipal level. According to Cloves Luiz Periera Oliviera, a member of the research group, 'A Cor da Bahia' (The Colour of Bahia), from the Federal University of Bahia, the majority of candidates for the state assembly did not seek the 'black vote', but merely wished to represent a given community, and defend a given ideology. Bahia's Regional Electoral Tribunal does not publish information on the ethnic or racial background of the candidates, but research conducted by Oliveira shows that 74 per cent of Salvador's population is comprised of Afro-Brazilians (*pretos* and *pardos*, or *mulatos*). In the municipal elections of 1992, 35.6 per cent of the candidates were white, 10.3 per cent *moreno* (a category which Oliveira distinguishes from white people and Afro-Brazilians) and 54.1 per cent Afro-Brazilian, so Afro-Brazilians were a majority of the candidates up for election.[102]

In 1992, 575 Afro-Brazilians competed against 377 white and 100 *moreno* candidates for 35 seats in the Municipal House of Assembly. Only 11.5 per cent of these candidates were women. The results of the elections are emblematic of the role of race in the political process. Only 34.4 per cent of all elected candidates were Afro-Brazilian. While this percentage indicates a disproportion between the number of Afro-Brazilian candidates and elected officials, it only tells part of the story. The figure represents an increase of more than 200 per cent from the 1988 elections, when Afro-Brazilians only represented 11.4 per cent of the elected candidates. Oliveira indicates that the majority of the elected candidates were men between the ages of 35 and 60, with a high level of education and usually from the upper middle class or middle class, but that more candidates from the working class were also elected (a total of 17 per cent). Gains by Afro-Brazilian women were slight.[103]

Oliveira also suggests that the advance of workers and Afro-Brazilians in the political arena may be because both groups feel less intimidated by prejudice and discrimination. But this view does not recognize that Afro-Brazilians have always been candidates for political posts. What has changed is a certain level of consciousness among both white people and black people which allows black candidates to win. The interrelationship between racial consciousness and political affiliation remains unclear, however. In Salvador, the PDT (Democratic Labour Party), PL (Liberal Party), PTB (Brazilian Workers' Party) and the PDC (Christian Democratic Party) fielded the largest number of candidates and also won the highest number of seats. Afro-Brazilians made up 50.6 per cent, 57.5 per cent, 52.6 per cent and 42.8 per cent of each party respectively. The Workers' Party (PT), the Workers' Party of Brazil (PTdoB) and the Popular Socialist Party (PPS), Social Democratic Party (PDS) and the Social Christian Party (PSC) fielded 64 per cent, 66.7 per cent, 66.7 per cent, 71.4 per cent and 74.3 per cent Afro-Brazilian candidates respectively. Only 5.8 per cent of PT candidates won, compared to less than 1 per cent of the PTDoB, 1 per cent of the PPS, 1 per cent of the PDS and 3.8 per cent of the PSC.[104]

The plethora of parties and the variation in outcome indicates another important issue. Brazilian parties have divided the Afro-Brazilian vote at the state and local level,

as they have at the national level. A number of liberal, ultra-liberal and moderate parties have many Afro-Brazilian candidates.[105]

Yedo Ferreira and Amauri Mendes Pereira warn that elections will not eliminate racism and that the black movement must always strive to be an independent force in the political arena.[106] The black movement is not monolithic, however, since it is comprised of many groups with diverging philosophies. People in the movement are right to be concerned since its force as an independent organization in the political realm has diminished considerably in the 1990s. There are two reasons for this. As individuals in the black movement became well known, they were invited by many parties to run for office. Once in the political realm, platforms inevitably expanded and racial questions become one issue on a list of issues of any given political platform. Another explanation, however, and perhaps a more important one, relates to the nature of the Brazilian political system. Unlike the United States, which has had a two-party system for most of its history, allowing a relatively coherent African-American community to align itself with one party against another to pursue economic, social and cultural advantage, in Brazil there are many parties that operate nationally and at state and municipal level. The existence of many political parties makes it difficult for Afro-Brazilians to rally around one candidate or party because of their stand on racial or human rights issues, diminishing the potential for racial solidarity.

Literacy, education and employment

In 1988, the IBGE reported that, as a general rule, black people have lower incomes live in poorer conditions and die earlier than white people. Afro-Brazilians have a 30 per cent higher infant mortality rate and are 50 per cent more likely to leave school without learning how to read. In the northeast, the infant mortality for Afro-Brazilians is as high as 96.3 per 1,000, compared to 68 for white people. Neither black nor white Brazilians are accustomed to explaining social disparities in racial terms, however, although they can readily discuss unequal class dynamics. Illusions of racial democracy still influence Brazilian social discourse, despite proof to the contrary – and despite special reports by mainstream magazines such as *Veja*, which reported in 1988 that slaves in the past were much better off than poor black people today.[107]

Socioeconomic indicators

Category	White	*Preto/Pardo*	Male	Female
Infant mortality (per 1,000 births)	37.3	62.3	48.0	36.4
Education level (out of 10)	6.2	4.2	5.2	5.0

Source: IBGE, Brazil, htp:/www.ibge.org and United Nations Educational, Scientific and Cultural Organization, htp:/www.un.org/Depts/unsd/social/literacy.ht (visited July 1999).

According to the IBGE, of the approximately 130 million Brazilians aged 5 or more, almost 35 million had no formal education or less than one year; some 29 million had between 1 and 3 years of education; almost 12 million had between 11 and 14 years of education; and only slightly more than 4 million had more than 15 years of education. In general, residents of urban areas have higher levels of education than those in rural areas. IBGE says that approximately 75 per cent of Brazilians are literate though other sources give a figure of 81 per cent, which is still low compared to other Latin American countries. Black and indigenous men have a slightly higher level of literacy than black women, although *parda* women indicate a higher level than *pardo* men. The ratio of white people who are literate compared to those who are illiterate is relatively high (5.4:1), meaning that the percentage of white illiteracy is low. For *pretos* and *pardos* that ratio is relatively low (1.8:1 and 1.9:1 respectively), indicating that more than half of Afro-Brazilians are illiterate.

Literacy in Brazil by gender and race, age 5 years or more

Categories	White	Black	*Pardo*	Indigenous
Total	56,708,392	4,376,301	36,626,732	109,243
Men	27,258,767	2,234,710	18,174,287	58,375
Women	29,449, 625	2,141,591	18,452,445	50,868

Source: *Censo Demográfico do Brasil*, 1991, pp. 192–7, Table 2.3 (rounded to 100th of a point).

Percentage of ethnic group or race with no formal education or less than one year

	Total	Female	Male
White people	19%	19%	19%
Pretos	36%	36%	36%
Pardos	35%	34%	36%
Indigenous	58%	60%	57%

Source: *Censo Demográfico do Brasil*, 1991, pp. 192–7, Table 2.3 (rounded to 100th of a point).

In addition to high illiteracy rates, few Afro-Brazilians have completed university studies. While various activists have called for affirmative action programmes to guarantee a given percentage of Afro-Brazilians in higher education, the reality is complicated by the examinations that Brazilians must take to secure a place at university and for many government positions. Only candidates with good secondary school preparation have a chance of being selected. Logically, candidates with more economic resources can go to private schools or can afford to take special classes to prepare for exams. Given the poor economic resources of the majority of Afro-Brazilians and the inadequate facilities in the public school system, Afro-Brazilians are clearly at a disadvantage. Statistics indicate that fewer than 1 per cent of Afro-Brazilian females and males complete higher education.

In general, Afro-Brazilians' employment is higher in state, local and national governmental positions than in the private sector. Afro-Brazilians are over-represented in lower-paying jobs such as custodial staff and guards, however, and in the informal economy. Many believe that discrimination is more acute in the private sector than in the public sector and statistics seem to bear this out. In the private sector, people say that racism is a problem of the market, since clients demand service from individuals with *boa aparencia* ('good appearance', a euphemism for 'No blacks need apply'). These superficial explanations allow companies and individuals to shrug off responsibility as if individuals cannot change or affect the marketplace. At the same time it is well known that Afro-Brazilian doctors, dentists and other professionals are routinely questioned about their competence by potential clients. One dentist reported that many potential clients did not even want to be touched by him.[108]

The public sector might seem more democratic since most positions are filled by examinations which do not ask a person's race or ethnic identity. Since Afro-Brazilian educational levels are significantly lower than those of white people, more Afro-Brazilians tend to apply for entry-level positions in the public sector than for management positions. Because of this, several grassroots initiatives have attempted to prepare students for the collge entrance exam, including the *Pre-Vestibular para Negros e Carentes* (College Preparatory Course for Black people and the Needy). The Conselho da Comunidade Negra (Black Community Council), a private company, has begun to design special courses for the black community.[109] The problem is that many applicants do not have sufficient funds to pay for these courses.

Getting a job in the public sector on the local, state or federal level does not necessarily mean that black people escape prejudice and discrimination. Many Afro-Brazilians complain that throughout their career they have been sidelined by white people for promotions. Eliza Argolo Benicio, with a university degree in law and now a public servant in Bahia, for example, believes that black people in the labour force 'attain what they have because they are black but also attain so little because they are black'. By that Benico means that there are many obstacles for black people and that to attain a good job, they have to work doubly hard.[110]

Labour force participation rate by sex and ethnic group, for population aged 15–65 (1996)

Region	Total	Male	Female	White	Afro-Brazilian°
Total	69.7	85.5	54.9	69.3	70.2
Urban North°°	67.0	83.1	51.9	67.1	67.0
Northeast	68.3	84.4	53.5	65.6	67.4
Southeast	68.8	84.8	53.8	68.0	70.6
South	74.8	88.9	61.2	74.7	76.0
Central-West	71.5	88.1	55.8	70.5	72.4

Notes: ° Includes *pardos* and *pretos*. °° Urban North does not include rural data from the states of Rondônia, Acre, Amazonas, Roraima and Pará.
Source: IBGE: http://www.ibge.org/english/e-index.html (visited July 1999).

Employment participation rates are higher for all population groups in the South and Southeast: 76.0 per cent and 70.6 per cent, respectively, shrinking to 67.4 per cent in the Northeast and 60.7 per cent in the urban North, though 'participation' may not mean that individuals have a full-time steady job, or a decent wage. Afro-Brazilian unemployment rates are consistently higher than those of white people in all regions, and the unemployment rate for females is consistently higher than that for males.

Unemployment rate by sex and ethnic group for population aged 15–65 (1996)

Brazil	Total	Male	Female	White	Afro-Brazilian°
Total	6.9	5.7	8.8	6.6	7.7
Urban North	7.7	6.0	10.2	6.8	8.2
Northeast	6.3	5.2	7.8	5.7	6.5
Southeast	7.7	6.2	9.8	7.4	8.7
South	5.4	4.5	6.6	5.1	8.1
Central-West	7.9	6.2	10.5	7.6	8.7

Note: ° Includes *pardos* and *pretos*.

Source: IBGE: http://www.ibge.org/english/e-index.html (visited July 1999).

Despite the economic and political problems of the current Brazilian government, Afro-Brazilian activists note that President Cardoso has appointed more Afro-Brazilians to top positions in his government than any other president in the history of Brazil. Aside from Pelé, who was named Minister of Sports, Carlos Alberto Reis de Paula from Minas Gerais became Ministro Togado do Tribunal Superior do Trabalho (Magistrate Minister of the Workers' Superior Tribunal), and Dulce Pereria, the current director of the Fundação Cultural Palmares, succeeded the well-known activist and teacher Joel Ruffino Santos. Still the Afro-Brazilian share of political power is relatively small, as is its economic power, despite the potential of the Afro-Brazilian consumer market.

Afro-Brazilians, property and land tenure

Agrarian reform remains a chronic problem, particularly in the North, the Northeast and the South of Brazil. The struggle for land by peasant land rights activists and indigenous groups has resulted in violence, death threats and assassinations of those most in need of land. In addition to its poor income distribution, Brazil has a poor land distribution, with a high percentage of land being owned by few people. According to the IBGE large landed estates (of 1,235 acres or more), which constitute 2 per cent of farms, account for half the total land in Brazil, most of it owned by absentee landowners. As a result, rural populations often have few ways of securing a subsistence living. According to the National Institute of Colonization and Agrarian Reform (INCRA), 1 per cent of the Brazilian population has control over 43 per cent of all productive land.[111]

Afro-Brazilians make up a substantial percentage of landless peasants struggling for lands, particularly in the Movimento dos Trabalhadores Rurais Sem Terra (Movement of Rural Workers without Land), but their struggle

is not framed in racial terms. It seems clear that landlessness in the North and Northeast extends across ethnic divides, and affects migrants and indigenous peoples disproportionately. It is also clear that rural life for Afro-Brazilians presents a different set of challenges from those of the city. Concomitant to the land struggle of peasants is the struggle by modern-day *quilombos*. Most of these are rural black communities with strong links to historical *quilombos*, or escaped-slave communities, although some, such as those in the state of Ceará, are comprised of *cafusos*, the progeny of indigenous people and black people.

According to the Fundação Cultural Palmares (Palmares Cultural Foundation), the body responsible for certifying modern-day *quilombos*, three criteria must be met: (1) the residents define themselves as such; (2) intellectuals and the local population must corroborate the claim; (3) public institutions from the state in which the *quilombo* is located must give their approval. Corroboration by the community will ensure that the *quilombos* receive titles for the lands which they presently occupy. This process is highly contentious and is complicated by the double role of the Fundação Cultural Palmares, which is responsible for rigorous governmental certification as well as for protecting the rights of the black community at large.[112]

Over 700 communities spread throughout the nation are hoping to be certified. According to the Fundação Palmares, as of September 1997, there were 571 proven *quilombos*, 511 of which had already been mapped out. These numbers are also controversial, however. According to Ivan Rodrigues da Costa of the National Commission of Quilobolas (residents of *quilombos*), in São Paulo alone there may be more than 400 communities and, if this is the case, the working number of 700 *quilombos* nationwide seems conservative.

Some communities, such as the *quilombo* of Boa Vista in the municipality of Oriximiná in Pará and Frechal in Mirinzal, Maranhão, have already received titles to the land, but many more impatiently await action from the government, since there is great tension between them and private landowners and farmers. Historically, landlessness and lack of jobs in rural areas has led to vagrancy and migration to urban centres. In urban centres, Afro-Brazilians make up the majority of the working class and of people living in *favelas* and in the street. They can also be found in disproportionate numbers in Brazil's prisons, and are the target of police and other institutional violence.

Afro-Brazilians, violence and the police

In Brazil, there are three distinct armed policing bodies: the state police, the military police and private security forces used by companies, institutions and some government buildings. While most Brazilians indicate that they fear the police, fear and mistrust are acute among certain groups including street children, homosexuals and Afro-Brazilians. Police officers routinely target these groups, but young black men, particularly in poor neighbourhoods or on public transport, are routinely stopped, searched and harassed.

The 1992 massacre of 111 prisoners in São Paulo's Curundiru Penitentiary, the majority of them Afro-Brazilians and many of them young and first-time offenders, is an indication of the violence directed at the Afro-Brazilian community. Prison officers tried to justify the killings on the grounds that they needed to establish order, since inmates had begun an uncontrollable riot. Many Brazilians were outraged at the massacre although, according to one poll cited by the *New York Times*, more than 40 per cent of Brazilians supported the police. Protests by human rights groups and prisoners led the governor of São Paulo, Luiz Antonio Fleury Jr, to dismiss the state's security director, Pedro Franco de Campos. Similar atrocities reported by international and national human rights groups from other areas have gone unnoticed, however.[113]

In 1997 the Inter-American Commission on Human Rights (IACHR) Report recommended widespread reforms of the state police forces. Police officers were responsible for an average of 20 deaths a month in 1996 alone, and in poor Afro-Brazilian communities, police are reportedly responsible for one-third of the deaths. The police's tough talk against crime, which is often supported by the elite and middle classes, means that suspects, innocent or guilty, often have no rights, and are abused by officers.

Because of stereotyping, black men are more likely to be arrested as suspects for both violent and non-violent crimes than any other population group. Although it is prohibited by the Federal Constitution, there are still cases of torture and inhuman treatment of suspects in prisons and in police stations. Between 1990 and 1997 the Public Prosecutor's Office in Belo Horizonte, Minas Gerais, for example, has indicted more than 500 police officers for a number of abuses.[114]

According to the northeastern NGO, the Luiz Freire Cultural Centre, of the 1,378 murder victims reported in Recife in 1994, 87 per cent were black. In São Paulo, the Nucleus for the Study of Violence reported that black people are more likely to receive tougher prison sentences than white people, whether they have lawyers or not. Many of the civil complaints are known to the government. President Cardoso, himself a supporter of human rights, has acknowledged these occurrences and has vowed not to keep this information secret.

As in other American communities, Afro-Brazilian representation in the police force is small. Furthermore, Afro-Brazilians in the rank and file often share the negative stereotypes held by the police force in general. In the summer of 1999, President Cardoso appointed Aglio Monteiro Filho, an Afro-Brazilian, to head the federal police. The former director was forced to resign after being accused of torturing prisoners during the military dictatorship. This appointment is important as reform is already under way – in September 1997, the Ministry of Justice created a new public security secretariat to reorganize the police forces. Monteiro Filho, who comes from the state of Minas Gerais, has been praised by human rights groups there, and by João Leite, a state deputy in Minas Gerais and chairman of the Human Rights Committee in the Minas Gerais Legislative Assembly.

Civil rights, ethnic rights, recognition and integration: Brazil and its record on human rights

Compared to many other nations, Brazil has an excellent record of ratifying international human rights instruments having signed up to many of the prominent conventions and treaties of the United Nations (UN) and Organization of American States (OAS), two major international organizations of which it is a part. In 1992 Brazil signed two important UN treaties: the International Covenant on Civil and Political Rights (ICCPR) and the International Covenant on Economic, Social and Cultural Rights (ICESCR). Between them, these two instruments underscore many rights outlined in the 1948 Universal Declaration of Human Rights including the prohibition of discrimination against individuals on any grounds, the right to education and work, as well as the right to self-determination which is provided for in Article 1 of both Covenants. As with many international human rights treaties, monitoring is done by the submission of state reports to the treaty monitoring body for assessment as to how the rights are being given effect. The ICCPR allows for individuals who feel they have had their rights violated to take their case to the UN Human Rights Committee, however Brazil has not signed the first optional protocol that would allow individuals access to this forum. Nor has Brazil signed the second optional protocol to the ICCPR which calls for the abolition of the death penalty, although Brazil currently has no death penalty.[115] The Brazilian government has ratified the Convention on the Rights of the Child (1990) but has not submitted their State Report – which was due in 1992 – to the Committee on the Rights of the Child.

Since 1948, Brazil has signed a number of other international treaties including the Convention on the Prevention and Punishment of the Crime of Genocide (15 April 1952), the Convention on Consent to Marriage, Minimum Age of Marriage and Registration of Marriage (11 February 1970), the Convention on the Rights of the Child (24 September 1990), the Convention on the Political Rights of Women (13 August 1963), the Convention on the Elimination of All Forms of Discrimination Against Women (31 March 1981), the International Convention on the Elimination of All Forms of Racial Discrimination (27 March 1968), and the Convention Against Torture and Other Cruel, Inhuman, or Degrading Treatment or Punishment (1989), in addition to the Universal Declaration of Human Rights of 1948.

Brazil's record is equally impressive in the Organization of American States, having signed the American Convention of Human Rights (20 June 1978), the Additional Protocol to the American Convention on Human Rights in the Area of Economic, Social and Cultural Rights (17 November 1988), the Protocol to the American Convention on Human Rights to Abolish the Death Penalty (7 June 1994), and various Inter-American conventions including the Convention to Prevent and Punish Torture (24 January 1986), the Convention on the International Traffic of Minors (18 March 1994), and the Convention on the Granting of Civil Rights to Women which dates back to 2 May 1948.[116]

Brazil's record was not so good on international accords prior to 1948. Brazil did not sign one of the earliest international instruments against slavery, the Slavery Convention of 9 March 1927, even though Brazil had officially abolished slavery in 1888. After the end of African slavery, many people of African descent remained in bondage through debts and poverty, and many immigrants worked as indentured servants, a practice which lasted well into the twentieth century. In 1992, Father Ricardo Rezende Figueira from the state of Pará, for example, presented a report to the United Nations documenting cases of slave labour involving more than 3,000 men, women and children. In many states, migrant workers are forced to work and live in slave-like conditions.[117] Thus, although Brazil has come a long way in terms of its international rhetoric on human rights, it needs to make a fuller commitment to enforcing the treaties that it has signed.

The 1988 Brazilian Constitution reflects a commitment to human rights and civil rights, and is intolerant of racism and social prejudice. The Constitution declares racial discrimination a federal crime, though few cases come to court. Still, the existence of laws that define both prejudice and discrimination as national crimes is an important step in Brazil, since prior to 1951 many Brazilians believed that such laws were unnecessary. Since the historic 1988 Constitution, the Brazilian government has better defined racism as a crime.

Section II, Law no. 7,716 of 5 January 1989, signed by President José Sarney, defined the crime of racism in 21 articles, guaranteeing Brazilian citizens that crimes of racial and colour prejudice 'shall be punished according to this law'. Moreover, this law defines racial and colour prejudice in twelve specific ways from 'impeding or obstructing access to any administrative position' to 'impeding marriage or familial or social living'. The law also defines specific penalties for each act of prejudice and discrimination, ranging from a minimum of two years to a maximum of five years imprisonment. Furthermore, Article 16 makes it possible for civil servants to lose their jobs or for business establishments to be shut down for no more than three months.[118] This law was further elaborated on 21 September 1990, when President Fernando Collor signed Law no. 8,081, which established the crimes and penalties for acts of discrimination and prejudice practised by the media.

On 13 May 1997, the Brazilian Congress amended Law no. 7,716 with Law no. 9,459 and changed the Penal Code (Decree-Law no. 2,848 of December 1940 which remained unaltered in the 1988 Constitution). This modification effectively amended Article 1 from 'The crimes of colour or racial prejudice shall be punished according to law', to 'The crimes of discrimination or prejudice according to race, colour, ethnicity, religion or national origin...'. In addition, Article 20 emphasizes that 'To practise, induce or initiate any type of discrimination or prejudice according to race, colour, ethnicity, or religion will carry a penalty of three years and a fine.' Congress also modified the Penal Code, to impose a penalty of imprisonment for three years and a fine for such an offence.[119]

Besides the aforementioned laws, Brazilians have other laws indicating a legal awareness of the value of civil and human rights. Among the most important of these are Law no. 8,069 of 13 July 1990, which legalized the 'Statutes of the Child and of the Adolescent'; Law no. 7,668 of 22 August 1988, which created the Palmares Cultural Foundation; Law no. 8,078 of 9 September 1990, which instituted the 'Code for the Defence of the Consumer', and Law no. 9,455 of 7 April 1997 which defines torture as a crime (Articles 1 and 2).

The government of Fernando Henrique Cardoso has an impressive record of establishing forums for discussion of civil and human rights on paper. It was Cardoso's government which created the National Programme for Human Rights in 1995, along with a number of other federal institutions. With help from the Ministry of Justice, UNESCO (Brazil) has also begun to play an important role in the monitoring of human rights and in the implementation of the national programme. Compared to many western nations, Brazilian laws seem ideal, but few people are familiar with the law, and fewer Brazilians see the law as important, partly due to the general belief that police officers, government officials and others in power are immune from the law. Indeed, it is clear that, as in other parts of the world, laws do not eliminate racism or discrimination – but they should provide a legitimate process for redress and thus serve both as a moral yardstick and a deterrent. Although some activists rightly view these initiatives with scepticism, their existence is nonetheless historic. Still, the government needs to be much more pro-active and determined to actually effect change.

Many Brazilians have not really come to grips with Brazil's violent history and the continued violence that the legacy of slavery and racism has engendered. While Afro-Brazilians have systematically been victims of brutality and violence by people in authority, society only reacts with indignation when such practices affect victims from the middle class or the elite. The massacre of Afro-Brazilians in prison or the killing of street children has engendered much debate because of its scale and international media coverage, but countless cases of violence against minorities, homosexuals and women continue unnoticed.[120]

Afro-Brazilians who have suffered discrimination at work or in other public arenas often do not report the incidents for fear of losing their job or future reprisals. Three examples reported in the 'Olho Vivo' column of the magazine *Raça Brasil* are indicative of the growing consciousness among Afro-Brazilians, who attempt to denounce racist behaviour. Each example illustrates that some Brazilians do not regard their racist behaviour as problematic; still, the fact that these denunciations come from ordinary citizens and not activists indicate that more Brazilians are becoming aware of their rights and are demanding that they be respected.

On 14 May 1998 during a Civil Law examination at the University Bandeirante in São Paulo, Marta Tomazi, a young white student accosted Maria Célia Benedito Mello, a 50-year-old black student. Ms Tomazi seemed irritated at the black women's presence and demanded that the attendance list be handed to her, remarking, 'Pass me the list, you black woman. That's why I don't like your race. You all should be lined up against a wall and shot. If it had been some years ago, I would have given you a whipping.'[121] Another case involved Marcel dos Santos Gerônimo, a coach from the São Paulo basketball team Pinheiros, who publicly shouted a number of racial slurs at Almir dos Santos Gerónimo, a black player from Rio's Flamengo basketball team.[122] In September of 1997, *Raça Brasil* reported a case where a high school teacher, Andrea Regiane dos Santos, had insulted the coordinator of the night classes, Maria Tereza Minossi, who was married to a black teacher at the school. Ms dos Santos, who disagreed with the way the coordinator had decided to charge students for copies in the school remarked to her class, which was made up of many Afro-Brazilians: 'She hooked up with a black and see what happens.'[123] These are but three published examples of thousands of complaints, many of which are reported but never reach the courts. All three cases involve public verbal insults in front of witnesses. They did not necessarily cause the loss of job, or result in injury or physical violence, but they were direct assaults which aimed at undermining each individual's job performance and civil status. All three victims filed formal complaints with the police department, all of which resulted in penalties, fines or warnings.

That the perpetrators in all of these cases used such derogatory remarks in public demonstrates how racial slurs or jokes are seen as a natural part of the Brazilian social fabric. Just as alarming are statements by police and other authorities who use terms such as 'looking suspicious' or having a 'thief's face', or 'something looks out of place' to refer to a black person's presence.[124] Even white Brazilians who consider themselves progressive use terms such as *negão*, *preto velho* or *ganga velha* to refer to acquaintances and sometimes even friends.[125] Still, it would be wrong to consider these terms in and of themselves pejorative. In both Spanish and Portuguese racial terms such as '*negro*' or '*negra*' (or the Brazilian '*nega*') may be used as terms of endearment.

The case of Congressman Remi Trinta (PL-MA),who verbally assaulted Sergio Arquimedes Pacheco da Cruz, a 43-year-old pilot on board an aircraft in the airport in the city of Belem is more disconcerting, however, since it involves a high-ranking public official. Trinta told Cruz that he 'had an inferiority complex because of his black skin', and went on to say that 'All black people are like that' in the presence of many witnesses. The case caused a stir in Congress and resulted in an unprecedented discussion of racism in the Comissão de Constituição e Justição e Redação (CCJR) but it did not result in the congressman's resignation or a public apology, as it would in many other countries.[126]

When activists call attention to racist behavior, many Brazilians defend themselves, declaring, as one Brazilian noted, 'I cannot possibly be racist, my mother is black.' Indeed João Garcia, a radio announcer at Radio Bandeirantes of Porto Alegre, who criticized a black umpire by remarking 'Let's see if he screws up at the beginning or at the end' (paraphrasing the racist saying 'Blacks, if they don't screw up in the beginning, they'll do it at the end'), stated that he was not racist because his wife was black.[127]

These responses indicate that Brazilians distinguish a 'general sense of prejudice for groups' from individual social behaviour, and that, as previously noted, prejudice or discriminatory behavior may not necessarily inhibit inter-racial social activities or even intimacy.

In his important work on cases of discrimination and the criminal justice system, António Sérgio Alfredo Guimarães correctly reports that all of the racial crimes in Brazil relate to restrictive or segregating practices which are difficult to prove in Brazilian society. According to Guimarães most racial offences in Brazil are of three types:

1. discrimination against someone when their colour or appearance makes them a suspect of a crime or some anti-social behavior which they have not committed; or

2. when someone's racial or ethnic condition is used to diminish his/her authority or to demoralize him/her or to inhibit him/her from carrying out a public function or some job or task; or

3. a racial slander is used as a way to deny or not recognize someone's social position, limiting his/her ability in the execution or performance of his/her job in public or social life.

While these cases may represent the majority of reported cases in Brazil, racial violence is not as uncommon as one might think.[128]

Guimarães' research illustrates how many of the racial offences against Afro-Brazilians are thrown into doubt by the perpetrators, the police and judges handling individual cases. Furthermore, many of the offences reported to police cannot be prosecuted because they represent 'per-sonal offences against one's honour' which are not covered by the law. This loophole allows both the police and judges to under-estimate the number of serious cases reported. Cases reported by women are particularly likely to be categorized as 'offences against personal honour' rather than crimes of prejudice or discrimination. According to Guimarães, 84 per cent of cases of discrimination reported by women were classified in this way by the authorities. Since 1995, offences against personal honour have been handled by special police stations, and are not usually treated as a criminal offences. One study conducted in São Paulo, however, indicated that Afro-Brazilians are victims of 80.4 per cent of such crimes.

Curiously, six Brazilians who identified themselves as white, reported offences which ridiculed the individuals' dark complexion, or an ancestor who was black.[129]

Using cases reported in major Brazilian newspapers, Guimarães has attempted to determine whether racial discrimination occurs more often in areas of higher population density or those with higher percentages of black people. It is difficult to determine to what extent the cases are representative of particular places, nonetheless the figures provide us with a point of comparison of 'cases reported in major newspapers' compared to the black population.

Cases of discrimination (reported in newspapers) per 100,000 black inhabitants

Metropolitan area	% of black people in the population	No. of cases reported in newspapers per 100,000 black inhabitants
Rio de Janeiro	10.5	5.55
São Paulo	4.6	6.5
Salvador	15.6	4.23
Belo Horizonte	8.3	5.78
Porto Alegre	6.0	5.91
Recife	5.6	2.43
Brasília	3.7	11.51
Curitiba	2.5	9.87
Belém	2.6	4.05
Fortaleza	2.0	0.00

Source: António Sérgio Alfredo Guimarães, *Preconceito e discriminação: Queixas de ofensas e tratamento desigual dos negros no Brasil*, Salvador, Bahia, Novas Toques, 1988, p. 105.

Guimarães suggests that Brasilia, Curitiba and São Paulo have the highest number of cases of discrimination in relation to the number of black inhabitants. However, this hypothesis must be treated with some caution. It may be more correct to suggest that in places such as Brasilia and Curitiba the black population publicizes acts of racial discrimination more forcefully, and the city newspapers are more likely to publish such stories. Nonetheless, other research is beginning to confirm what many Afro-Brazilians have known for a long time: that they do not have equal access to the law. Black defendants cannot afford legal assistance, and many do not know their rights. As a general rule black people receive tougher sentences than white ones. Many in the black movement therefore continue to fight for equal rights in all sectors of Brazilian society.

Children and education: the future

In all the social indicators, Afro-Brazilian children, like their elders, are most disadvantaged. Poverty, poor education and lack of role models all contribute to the many problems facing Afro-Brazilian children and adolescents. If adult rights are not respected, securing children's rights is even more problematic. During the 1990s, various human rights organizations have protested at the torture, abuse and murder of children, particularly in urban areas. According to the Public Ministry, for example, between 1988 and 1991, 5,644 youngsters between the ages of 5 and 17 were victims of violent deaths. In 1994 Human Rights Watch reported that children were routinely murdered by police and paramilitary groups, but 'what has come to be known as killing of children is, in the majority of cases, the killing of male adolescents, fourteen to seventeen years of age, a disproportionate share of whom are black'.[130]

Of all the homicides of minors from 1988 to 1990, 82 per cent were black boys. In São Paulo, the Afro-Brazilian homicide rate is disproportionately high, accounting for 51.7 per cent of the victims, according to the Centre for the Study of Violence (NEV) at the University of São Paulo. All of those killed were not street children, nor were they all killed by police or paramilitary forces, but the statistic partly explains Afro-Brazilians' fear of the police. Almost all of the victims are poor and, according to some reports, class considerations outweigh racial ones.[131]

The 1993 killings of eight children sleeping in the streets of the city of Rio de Janeiro, known as the 'Candelaria Massacre', created a public uproar and re-assessment of Brazilian laws which protect children. Many Brazilians, however (influenced by sensationalist depictions of street children in the media), view Afro-Brazilian victims as vagrants thus justifying harsh treatment and even their extermination. Countless stories of violence against Afro-Brazilian young men – harassment on buses, impromptu searches and beatings – can be recounted by residents from the *favelas* of Rio, São Paulo or Salvador, three of the nation's largest cities. All this despite Brazil's passing of the 1990 Estatuto da Criança e do Adolocente (Statute of the Child and the Adolescent).

Since the First National Congress of Street Children in Brasilia in 1986, a number of organizations and activists have struggled to bring attention to the plight of street children, among them the Movimento Nacional de Meninos e Meninas da Rua (National Movement of Street Children, or MNMMR), the Núcleo de Estudos da Violencia (Nucleus for the Study of Violence, or NEV) and Instituto Brasileiro de Análisis Socias e Econômicas (Brazilian Institute for Social and Economic Analysis, or IBASE). As a result Brazil was one of the first countries to ratify the Convention on the Rights of the Child, and used its 1988 constitutional debates to include many of the principles of the UN Convention on the Rights of the Child in its Constitution. Implementation of the laws is more difficult than establishing them, however, and Brazil's enforcement lags far behind.[132]

While the government must enforce the laws of the land, activists working in the community and in the field of education continue to forge a dialogue on human rights and the rights of children in an effort to foster a culture where human rights are universally known and accepted, and where abuses are routinely reported. In this regard, the Ministry of Education is beginning to play a crucial role since the release of the 'Parâmetros Curriculares Nacionais' (National Curricular Parameters, or PCN) in 1997. The principles of the PCN reflect years of work by educators committed to ideas of participatory citizenship and encouraging respect for cultural plurality.

According to Betty Mindlin, coordinator of the Institute of Anthropology and the Environment and a human rights advocate, the PCN will forge a vision of the world in which citizenship, social justice, appreciation of cultural diversity, human rights, and participation in all public and collective decisions are fundamental. The PCN is particularly innovative in the area of cultural plurality, as it encourages a positive affirmation of cultural diversity as 'a human treasure to be explored, as a source of knowledge and research to be used in all of the disciplines', rather than turning cultural plurality into a folkloric curiosity.[133] Over the next decades new Brazilian texts will help to promote this new vision. Publications such as *Sou Criança: Tenho Direitos*, for example, already provide pedagogical guides for introducing human rights into primary schools. The publication's simple philosophy of 'Seeing, knowing, celebrating and committing' has already received praise from educators, but the publication is still unknown to many teachers in impoverished areas of Brazil.

Moreover, as the magazine *Educação* has demonstrated, many teachers continue to treat black students like second-class citizens in class. Singer Gilberto Gil remembers, not without pain, that as a schoolboy a teacher called him 'a black boy with a big mouth', and asked him to keep quiet in class. That was at least two generations ago, but such behaviour continues today. According to Eliana Cavalleiro, a researcher from the Department of Education at the University of São Paulo, the biggest problem is that many teachers still do not admit that racial prejudice and discrimination exist in Brazil. This conclusion has been confirmed by various studies indicating that both students and teachers believe that among themselves prejudice does not exist. In reality, many students are afraid to expose their own prejudices and often go to great lengths to hide their own differences and poor living conditions. The myth of racial democracy continues to exist, despite research results to the contrary.[134]

Alternative educational programmes such as those instituted by Ilê Ayê have begun to play an important role in the education of children. With the help of educators, Ilê Ayê has developed and published a number of educational texts which highlight the role of Afro-Brazilians in history and society. These texts are more elaborate extensions of Ilê Ayê's musical compositions, aiming to educate young people. Schools such as Mãe Hilda in Liberdade, named after one of the original founders of the group and a *Candomblé* priestess, provide positive grassroots models for the entire nation.

There are few children's books which focus on Afro-Brazilian themes, and young people have few resources to turn to when they have questions about racial identity, slavery, African culture or religion. Heloisa Pires Lima's

Histórias da Preta, which includes stories about Africa, racial terminology, *Candomblé* and other Afro-Brazilian cultural traditions, Maria Aparecida da Silva and Silva Bento Cidania's *Em Preto e Branco: Discutindo as Relações Racias*, and Júlio Emílio Braz's *Felicidade Não Tem Cor* are three examples.[135] Advertisements for others occasionally appear in magazines such as *Raça* and *Black People,* but these publications are difficult to acquire despite their importance.

One project that will bear fruit in the future involves the private sector, the government and the activist community called Generação XXI (Generation 21). The goal of the programme is simple: to prepare young black adolescents to enter the twentieth century as productive citizens. The BankBoston has committed financial resources and time for the next nine years to ensure that 21 of São Paulo's black youngsters will carry on with their studies. The programme provides students with scholarships, transport, allowances for food, and medical and dental insurance, all of which they would normally lack. According to Maria Aparecida da Silva, director of the project, without this support most of the students would be forced to leave school and work in low-paying jobs in the city. In addition to the financial support which allows them to focus on their studies, students also participate in a number of forums such as after-school classes and talks which often include parents and members of the community. Employees of the BankBoston are encouraged to collaborate on various projects that benefit the students.[136]

The Generation XXI project is an important initiative that will serve as a model for the future. Organizers hope to show that once resources are invested in black communities, Afro-Brazilians will prosper. At the same time, progressive companies such as the BankBoston have demonstrated that they believe the business community has a fundamental commitment to large social issues in the community. The project is, in some respects, a small example of affirmative action at work in Brazil, since it recognizes the especially precarious situation of poor black students within a large percentage of Brazilians who are not able to complete secondary school.[137]

In September 1997, a special working group on discrimination issued 29 recommendations to the government, many of them controversial (the creation of affirmative action programmes in the universities and in government hiring, for example). While the president acknowledges the need for such programmes, to date, official affirmative action programmes remain too problematic and too politically sensitive to implement.

Conclusion

This report has presented a number of important social, economic and cultural indicators of Afro-Brazilians. Afro-Brazilians and their allies have much to campaign around but there is also some reason for cautious optimism.

To the question 'Who are the Afro-Brazilians and how have they contributed to the continued development of Brazilian society?' this report has given several answers. First, Afro-Brazilians are not a monolithic group. Like other Brazilian ethnic groups, they identify themselves by their regions. In addition, Afro-Brazilians have inherited a cultural system which has historically distinguished people by skin colour. Although the majority of Africans entered Brazil in a socially inferior position, Africans and their descendants have helped create Brazilian culture. Their influence in the arts and music, architecture, food, language and religion are undeniable.

To the question, 'How have they been marginalized (and continue to be marginalized) from mainstream Brazilian society?' we have seen that, despite their contribution, discrimination against Afro-Brazilians is endemic even in areas such as the Northeast where they constitute a majority of the population

Despite official government policies, most ethnic socioeconomic indicators reveal a sharp distinction between white Brazilians and Afro-Brazilians. While statistics vary from region to region, on a national scale Afro-Brazilians are more economically disadvantaged, have higher unemployment rates, lower levels of education and higher infant mortality than white Brazilians, although they fare better than the indigenous peoples.

From the nineteenth century, the Brazilian elite tried to attract European immigrants, so as to whiten the Brazilian population and present what they believed to be a modern image, free of the legacy of slavery. Until very recently, Brazil systematically avoided presenting images of Afro-Brazilians as national symbols. Today, Afro-Brazilians are drastically under-represented in all top or middle management professions, on television and in the cinema, and in the media at large. They are over-represented in poorly paid jobs, in the *favelas* and in prisons. Of the small number of Afro-Brazilians who have overcome the obstacles and obtained a good education, many have found professional life challenging because of their race. Brazilian employers harbour prejudices and stereotypes about black people which allow them to deny opportunities to well-qualified Afro-Brazilians in many professions. At the same time, the myth of racial democracy remains a very potent ideology, and many Brazilians, white and black, will say that there is no racial prejudice in Brazil. As evidence, Brazilians will note specific examples such as Pelé, or talk of widespread miscegenation, assumptions that inter-racial sexual relations somehow diminish racial prejudice. Still, it is true that Brazilians intermingle across social, ethnic and class lines with ease and tolerance, unlike Europeans or North Americans.[138]

Some Afro-Brazilians have fared quite well in Brazilian society, particularly in the fields of entertainment and sports. But often Afro-Brazilians have to demonstrate exceptional talent in order to gain attention. Indeed, as Michael Hanchard explains in *Orpheus and Power*, black exceptionalism allows many Brazilians to hold on to the myth of racial democracy.[139] Many Brazilians continue to explain away racial prejudice as class prejudice. It is true that the majority of Afro-Brazilians are poor, but it is not true that the few upwardly mobile black people are free from discrimination.

And what have Afro-Brazilians and their allies done to combat their disenfranchisement? This report began with a survey of Brazilian history paying special attention to the efforts Afro-Brazilians to challenge racism and to secure their civil and human rights. Hanchard and others have argued that the black movement has often focused attention on cultural activities, rather than pressing for political and economic rights. But these observations must be carefully contextualized both nationally and regionally. Brazil lacks a strong democratic tradition, having a monarchy for most of the nineteenth century, then a corrupt republic that cared little for the masses and, in the twentieth century, a dictatorship which blocked grassroots movements for decades. Furthermore, the unique system of political and economic patronage in place in Brazil has traditionally worked against autonomous challenges to the status quo (particularly when we consider that few Afro-Brazilian politicians have been elected to places where they can affect legislation). Still, many regional and local groups have called for change on a national and local level. In some instances cultural activities served as important political venues. In others, music, art and theatre played an important role in education and consciousness-raising. However, political and economic disenfranchisement, coupled with strong patriotic tendencies and continued belief in the myths of Brazilian racial democracy have historically made it difficult for Afro-Brazilians to galvanize mass support. This may change in the future, however.

On a national level, the black movement has helped to institutionalize important historical dates to encourage Brazilians of all backgrounds to reflect on their cultural ancestry, on race relations and on the plight of minorities in Brazil. Where previously the government had designated 13 May, the date of the signing of the Golden Law which gave freedom to all Brazilian slaves as an Afro-Brazilian holiday, activists have institutionalized 20 November, the anniversary of the death of Zumbi, the famed leader of Palmares, as an important moment for reflection and protest, now called the Day of Black Consciousness.

In celebrating the 500th anniversary of the arrival of the Portuguese in South America, it is important to remember that colonization was based on the subjugation of African and indigenous people and their descendants. Despite this, Afro-Brazilians have made great contributions to Brazilian culture, although these are not always recognized. It is time for the recognition of Afro-Brazilians as full citizens, which means equal access to educational and cultural opportunities, and economic and political ones as well.

Recommendations

1. Addressing structural inequalities

The Brazilian government should urgently prioritize special measures to facilitate the full participation of minority and indigenous groups in all aspects of political, economic, social and cultural life, as enshrined in the UN Declaration on the Rights of Persons belonging to National, Ethnic, Religious and Linguistic Minorities and in article 2.2 of the Convention on the Elimination of All Forms of Racial Discrimination. Particular consideration should be given to discrimination and marginalization in access to employment, land tenure, the right to health and shelter, and law enforcement.

2. Domestic legislation and international human rights standards

The Brazilian government should urgently enforce the provisions of the 1988 Constitution and the extensive complementary legislation for the protection of human rights. It should strengthen the independence and impartiality of public officials, especially for the judiciary and others working in the criminal justice system, to ensure that all act in consistency with international human rights standards. Priority should be given to upholding obligations under international law to protect the right to life and the right to a fair trial as stated in the ICCPR and the widespread prohibition on discrimination. The government should foster general public education in the understanding of human rights and the means by which they may be promoted.

3. Protection of Afro-Brazilian children

The Brazilian government should address the fundamental human rights of its many hundreds of thousands of street children, the majority of whom are Afro-Brazilian. The immediate submission to the Committee on the Rights of the Child of the Brazilian state report under the Convention on the Rights of the Child, which was due in 1992, is strongly urged. Action should be taken to implement the 1997 recommendations of the Inter-American Commission on Human Rights concerning reforms of the state and police forces.

4. Education: access and content

To remedy long-standing discrimination against Afro-Brazilian children and young adults in the education system, the government needs to ensure equality of access and greater equality of outcomes. Special provisions in the form of scholarships, internships, targeted training and special educational programmes are required on a wide scale and should be geared to promoting understanding of Afro-Brazilian cultural identity and fostering intercultural respect.

5. Responsibility in the media

The Brazilian media has a responsibility to promote equality and non-discrimination in its coverage of events and national life. The government and media should prioritize the elimination of inaccurate and stereotypical coverage of Afro-Brazilians and their culture. Programming should aim to promote respect for Afro-Brazilian and other minority cultures and to highlight their contribution to Brazil. Hiring policies in the media should promote representational participation.

6. Implementing affirmative action

MRG urges the immediate implementation by the Brazilian government of the recommendations of the National Programme for Human Rights (Programa Nacional de Direitos Humanos) for the promotion of affirmative action initiatives in both the public and private sectors to address entrenched inequalities.

7. International and intergovernmental actors and economic development

Transnational corporations investing in Brazil have a responsibility to ensure that their activities promote wider opportunity and greater equality of outcomes across the ethnic divide rather than reinforcing existing patterns of injustice. Intergovernmetnal bodies such as the UN and the OAS should hold corporations accountable for the impact of their actions on local communities. International financial institutions such as the World Bank and Inter-American Development Bank should support projects based on genuine consultation with and impacting favourably on, Afro-Brazilians and other marginalized communities.

8. Advocacy in international fora

International non-governmental organizations should support their Brazilian counterparts in consolidating strategies to raise and address issues of racism through such international fora as the World Conference on Racism (Year 2001) and the UN Sub-Commission on the Promotion and Protection of Human Rights.

1   'O Branco Selvajem', *Veja*, 11 May 1998, p. 36.
2   The Brazilian spelling *mulato* is italicized throughout the text, while the English spelling mulatto is not.
3   Araújo, E. (ed.), *A Mão Afro-Brasileira: Significado da Contribuição Artistica e Histórica*, São Paulo, Tenenge, 1988.
4   See Gilberto Gil, 'A mão da limpeza' (literally 'The hand that cleans') from his album *Raça Humana* (The Human Race) 1984.
5   See Kent, R.K., 'An African state in Brazil', in Richard Price (ed.) *Maroon Societies*, New York, Anchor Books, 1973, pp. 170–90.
6   Bethel, L., *Colonial Brazil*, Cambridge, Cambridge University Press, 1987, p. 86.
7   Of ten major *quilombos* formed in colonial Brazil, seven were destroyed within two years of being formed. Carlota Mato Grosso was wiped out after existing for 25 years, from 1770 to 1795.
8   Kent, *op. cit.*, p. 176, points to the presence of the indigenous people and the Portuguese values that some of the slaves had already adopted.
9   Price, R., *Maroon Societies*, New York, Anchor Books, 1973, p. 169.
10 Lopes, Nei, 'As linguas dos povos Bantos e o Português no Brasil', *Revista do Patrimônio Histórico e Arístico Nacional* no. 25, 1997, pp. 269–78.
11 Moises, J.A., 'Constituinte e direitos humanos', in M.R. Abreu (ed.) *Constituição e Constituinte*, Brasilia, Editora Universidad de Brasilia, 1987, p. 42.
12 Rankin, J., *Letters on American Slavery*, Letter 2, New York, Arno Press, 1969, pp. 14–19.
13 *Constituições Brasileiras*, São Paulo, Sugestões Literárias, S/A, 1978, p. 550. Don Pedro wrote most of the Constitution of 1824 after dissolving the elected assembly.
14 Nabuco, J., *Abolitionism: The Brazilian Anti-Slavery Struggle*, Urbana, Chicago and London, University of Chicago Press, 1977, p. 223.
15 Skidmore, T.E., 'Racial ideas and social policy in Brazil 1870–1940', in R. Graham (ed.) *The Idea of Race in Latin America*, Austin, University of Texas Press, 1990, p. 9.
16 Nabuco, *op. cit.*, p. 21.
17 Bento, C.M., *O Negro e Decendentes no Sociedade do Rio Grande do Sul 1635–1975*, Porto Alegre, Grafosul, 1976, p. 246.
18 *Constituições Brasileiras*, p. 550. For a discussion of the Constitution of 1824 during the creation of the 1988 Constitution see A.M. Viera do Rosario, 'A Constituinte de 1823 e a Constitução de 1824', in Abreu, *Constituição e Constituinte*, p. 26.
19 *Constituições Brasileiras*, p. 517. President Deodoro da Fonseca created a commission of five members to elaborate the Constitution.
20 Hasenbalg, C., *Descriminação e Desigualdade Racias no Brasil*, Rio de Janeiro, Graal, 1979, pp. 256–9.
21 During the war, the state conscripted many slaves into the army in exchange for a promise of freedom. Others were 'donated' by their owners.
22 Nachman, R.G., 'Positivism, modernization and the middle class in Brazil', *Hispanic American Historical Review*, vol. 57, no. 7, 1977, pp. 1–23. Kim Butler also discusses the role of order in *Freedoms Given, Freedoms Won: Afro-Brazilians in Post-Abolition São Paulo and Salvador*, New Brunswick, NJ, Rutgers University Press, 1998.
23 Ibid., pp. 15–16.
24 See Hall Stauffer, D., 'The origins and establishment of Brazil's Indian Service: 1889–1910', Diss., University of Texas, 1956.
25 Several documents have left rich sources of information for regional studies. Magazines and newspapers with such names as *O Bandeirante*, *Senzala* and *Libertade* attempted to address national issues as they related to black people.
26 Bradford Burns, E., 'The destruction of a folk past: Euclides Da Cunha and cataclysmic cultural clash', *Review of Latin American Studies*, vol. 3, no. 1, 1990, pp. 16–35.
27 Coelho, J.G.L., 'Breves anotacões sobre a Constituição de 1934', in Abreu, *Constituição e Constituinte*, p. 27. National education was still an embarrassment, however, owing to its blatant disregard for the understanding of the Afro-Brazilian reality. Do Nascimento, A., *Povo Negro: A Sucessão e a Nova Republica*, Rio de Janeiro, IPEAFRO, 1985, p. 25.
28 *Constituições Brasileiras*, p. 447.
29 Skidmore, *op. cit.*, pp. 7–36.
30 Sodré, N.W., *Síntese de Historia da Cultura Brasileira*, 8th edn, Rio de Janeiro, Civilização Brasileira, 1980.
31 From Frank Tannenbaum's introduction to Freyre, G., *The Mansions and the Shanties: The Making of Modern Brazil*, New York, Alfred A. Knopf, 1963.
32 Ibid., p. 7.
33 Franco, J., *The Modern Culture of Latin America: Society and the Artist*, Middlesex, England, Pelican Books, 1967.
34 'Nós e Katherine Dunham', *Quilombo*, vol. 2. nos 7–8 (March–April), p. 11. Also see interview with Katherine Dunham by Yvonne Jean published in *Correio da Manhã*, June 1950, suppl. p. 9. The incident of discrimination against Ms Duncan apparently had to do with the mix up of her hotel reservation. It was never determined whether the error by the hotel was intentional or not.
35 'Nós e a Frente Negra Brazileira', *O Clarim d'Alvorada*, 23 September 1931, p. 2. 'Estatutos da Frente Negra Brasileira', *A Voz da Raça*, May 1937. Mello, V., *1978–1988: 10 Anos de Luta Contra o Racismo*, Salvador, Movimento Negro Unificado, 1988, pp. 64–79. See also Moura, C., *Brasil: As Raizes do Protesta Negro*, São Paulo, Editora Global, 1983. Moura provides a good description of the black movement in the state of São Paulo using primary sources and interviews.
36 Lucrécio, F., 'Memoria histórica a Frente Negra Brasileira', no publisher, pp. 332–42. See also Lucrécio, F., 'A constante fundação de núcleos frentenegrinos', *A Voz da Raça*, September 1936.
37 Yglesias, F., 'A Constituição de 1937', in Abreu, *Constituição e Constituinte*, p. 28.
38 *Constituições Brasileiras*, p. 375, Article 122.
39 Skidmore, T.E. *Politics in Brazil 1930–1964: An Experiment in Democracy*, New York, Oxford University Press, 1967, pp. 28-30.

AFRO-BRAZILIANS: TIME FOR RECOGNITION

40   *Constituição dos Estados Unidos do Brasil*, São Paulo, Livraria Academica, 1946.

41   'Nosso programa', *Quilombo*, vol. 1, no. 1, Dec. 1948, p. 3.

42   Ibid., pp. 1–17 and pp. 97–137.

43   'Noticias de TEN', *Quilombo*, vol. 1, no. 2, Dec. 1948, p. 7.

44   Do Nascimento, A., 'Epiritú e fisonomia do TEN' (Discourse given at the opening of the National Negro Congress, 9 May 1949) reprinted in *Quilombo*, vol. 1, no. 4, May 1949, p. 11.

45   *Quilombo*, vol. 1, no. 1, Dec. 1948, p. 4. Costa also named several private schools including Notre Dame de Sion which refused to accept black children.

46   *Quilombo*, vol. 1, no. 1, Dec. 1948, p. 4. The Ministry of Education routinely provided funding to other theatrical and education-related groups. Various politicians such as Mendes de Morais, from the Prefeitura promised funding but it never came through. TEN also waited to see if the promise made by Café Filho, Rio de Janeiro Congressman, would materialize.

47   Do Nascimento M., 'Crianças racistas', 'Fala mulher', *Quilombo*, vol. 1, no. 1, Dec. 1948, last page.

48   'Instalado a Conselho Nacional das Mulheres Negras', *Quilombo*, vol. 2, nos 7–8, March–April 1950, p. 4.

49   'O negro e a eleições', *Quilombo*, vol. 2, no. 5, Jan. 1950, p. 3 and 'Ministro, senadores e diplomátas negros', *Quilombo*, vol. 2, no. 5, Jan. 1950, p. 8.

50   *Constituições Brasileiras*, pp. 13–23.

51   Ibid., p. 58.

52   Ato Institucional 5/1968, *Constituições Brasileiras*, pp. 59–60.

53   Ibid., p. 58.

54   Fernandes, F., *The Negro in Brazilian Society*, trans. Jacqueline D. Skiles et al., Atheneum and New York, Columbia University Press, 1969. Original book entitled *A Integração do Negro na Sociedade de Classes*, 1965.

55   Ibid., pp. 132–4.

56   Ibid.

57   In 1982, the electoral college chose provisional President Tancredo Neves who would lead Brazil back to democracy. Neves, who fell ill, was succeeded by his Vice President, José Sarney. The first popularly elected president, Fernando Collor de Mello, came to power in 1990.

58   Decreto no. 6627, 21 March 1983, instituted by the United Nations General Asembly in 1966.

59   The precursor to the MNU was the Movimento Unificado Contra a Discriminação Racial (MUCDR) which later added the word 'negro' becoming the MNUCDR.

60   Abdias do Nascimento, tape recorded interview, 16 May 1991, at Abdias do Nascimento's residence, Rio de Janeiro. Many of these items are reprinted in do Nascimento, *Povo Negro*, p. 25.

61   Sendao Federal, *Constituição da Republica Federal do Brasil*, Brasilia, 1991, p. 11.

62   Ibid., p. 23.

63   Ibid.

64   For a good overview of race relations in São Paulo see Andrews, G.R., *Blacks and Whites in São Paulo, 1888–1988*, Madison, University of Wisconsin Press, 1991.

65   Burdick, J., 'Brazil's black consciousness movement', *NACCLA Report on the Americas*, vol. 15, no. 4, pp. 23–7. The PT was led by Ignacio Lula da Silva, ex-president Collor's principal opponent in the 1989 election, while the PDT was led by the charismatic Rio politician Leonel Brizola.

66   'Deputado Federal, PDT' (political pamphlet), Rio de Janeiro, 1989.

67   Dos Santos, P.R., 'Conciência negra, conciência nacional', *Bandeirantes*, vol. 58, no. 6, p. 1.

68   www.minc.gov.br/fcp/sombre.htm (visited July 1999).

69   'Boletin II Encontro Nacional de Entidades Negras'. Tape recorded inverview with Sebastião Fortes, IPCN (Centro de Pesquisas das Culturas Negras), Rio de Janeiro, 24 June 1999.

70   'Letter from Minas Gerais', Communication published by IPCN, 1995.

71   PPPOMAR 'Da maioria, com maioria, pela maioria', *Afro-Reggae*, vol. 6, no. 35, pp. 4–5.

72   Interview with Sueli Carneiro, Director of Human Rights, Geledés, São Paulo, 29 June 1999.

73   See Cardoso, F.H. and Cardoso, O., *Cor e Mobilidade Social em Florionopolis: Aspectos as Relações entre Negros e Brancos Numa Comunidade do Brasil Meridonal*, São Paulo, Compañia Editora Nacional, 1960.

74   'Tirando o astraso, "negros em movimento"', *Raça Brasil*, June 1999, pp. 60–3.

75   Tape recorded interview with Nelson Mendes, Director of Olodum, 6 July 1999, Olodum Headquarters, Pelourinho, Salvador.

76   Tape recorded interview with Grupo Steve Biko, 9 June 1999, Salvador, Bahia.

77   Tape recorded interview at Iyalodê Centro de Estudos Orientais, UFBA, 5 July 1999, Salvador, Bahia.

78   Tape recorded interview, Asantawaa, 4 July 1999, Salvador, Bahia.

79   Interview. See also Djumbay's home page www.ocara.org.br/djumbay

80   Davis, J., *Avoiding the Dark: Race, Nation and National Culture in Modern Brazil*, Hampshire, UK, Ashgate Publishing Co., 1991.

81   Raphael, A., 'From popular culture to micro enterprise: the history of the Brazilian samba schools', *Latin American Music Review*, vol. 11, no. 1, June 1990, pp. 73–83.

82   Tape recorded interview with Vovô, Secretary of Bloco Carnavalesco Ilê Ayê, 2 July 1999, Salvador, Bahia.

83   Guerreiro, G., 'Uma mapa em preto e branco da musica Bahia – Territorialização e mestiçagem no meio musical de Salvador, 1987–1997', in Livio Sansone and Jocélio Teles dos Santaos (eds) *Ritmos em Trânsito: Sócio-Antropologia da Música Bahiana*, Salvador, Dynamics Editorial, 1998, pp. 91–122. Interview with Vovô, 2 July 1999; tape recorded interview with Ana Maria Célia, 4 July 1999, at her residence in Salvador da Bahia; interview with Eliza Benicio Argolo, UFB, 6 July 1999, Salvador, Bahia.

84   Guerreiro, *op. cit.*, p. 104.

85   Tape recorded interview with Nelson Mendes, 7 July 1999, Olodum Headquarters, Pelourinho, Salvador.

86   Tape recorded interview with Carlos Alberto Medeiros, sub-secretary of the Rio de Janeiro Secretariat for Human Rights, 8 July 1999, at the Headquarters of the

Secretariat of Human Rights, Rio de Janeiro. See also Hanchard, M.G., *Orpheus and Power: The Movimento Negro of Rio de Janeiro and São Paulo, Brazil, 1945–1988*, Princeton, NJ, Princeton University Press, 1994.

87 Quoted in *Pode Crê: Música, Política e Outras Coisas*, vol. 11, no. 4, p. 16. *Pode Crê* was an important product of the Programme of Human Rights/SOS Racismo and the Rappers' Project of the NGO Gelédes in São Paulo which has ceased to be published because of lack of resources.

88 Caetano Veloso and Gilberto Gil, 'Haiti' (1996).

89 'O general que odiava a si mesmo', *Irohin*, vol. 4, nos 4–5, p. 11.

90 *Censo Demográfico 1991: Características Gerais da Populaçao e Instrução*, Rio de Janeiro, IBGE, 1991, pp. 162–4.

91 Ibid., pp. 162–4.

92 Ibid., pp. 178–80.

93 Dzidzienyo, A. and Casal, L., *The Position of Blacks in Brazilian and Cuban Society*, London, MRG, 1979.

94 Do Nascimento, A., 'Discourse to a group of Brazilian students', Centre for Social and Political Studies (CESP), Rio de Janeiro, 8 July 1999.

95 See Rodrigues, J.C., *O Negro Brasileiro e o Cinema*, Rio de Janeiro, Globo, 1998. The author presents twelve major stereotypes of blacks present in Brazilian cinema.

96 Dzidzienyo and Casal, *op. cit.*

97 Ministério da Justiça, Secretaria Nacional dos Direitos Humanos, Brasilia and UNESCO-Universidade de São Paulo, *Direitos Humanos no Cotidiano*, Brasilia, Ministerio da Justiça, Secretaria dos Direitos Humanos, 1988, p. 178.

98 *Direitos Humanos no Cotidiano*, p. 178.

99 Dzidzienyo and Casal, *op.cit.*

100 Anecdotal evidence suggests that different perceptions of race between Brazilians and North Americans and Europeans has an impact on views on inter-racial couples in Brazil. What North Americans may regard as an inter-racial couple, may not be considered an inter-racial couple in Brazil: for instance, a light-skinned *afromestiça* with blue eyes and a dark mulatto.

101 Tape recorded interview with Maria Luiza Junior, Salvador, Bahia, 4 July 1999.

102 Oliveira, C.L.P., *A Luta por um Lugar: Gênero, Raça e Classe Elições Municipais de Salvador-Bahia*, 1992, Salvador, Bahia, Novos Toques (Programa Cor da Bahia), 1994, pp. 24–6.

103 Ibid., pp. 34–9.

104 Ibid., p. 81 and pp. 116–17.

105 Ibid., p. 81.

106 'Movimento Negro e as eleições', communication published by IPCN.

107 'Na segunda classe', *Veja*, May 1977, pp. 22–30.

108 Tape recorded interview with Maria Aparecida da Silva, Director of Generação XXI, São Paulo, Brazil, 19 June 1999.

109 See www.centraldeconsursos.com.br

110 'Aqui a cor não conta', *Raça*, November 1998, pp. 48–51. Tape recorded interview with Eliza Argola Benicio, Federal University of Bahia, 6 July 1999.

111 United Nations Development Programme, *Human Development Report 1991*, New York, Oxford University Press, 1991, p. 136. Human Rights Watch, *The Struggle for Land in Brazil: Rural Violence Continues*, New York, Washington, Los Angeles, London, Human Rights Watch, 1992, pp. 1–12, *Direitos Humanos no Cotidiano*, p. 190.

112 See *Raça*, September 1997, pp. 79–84.

113 Brooke, J., 'Brazil's police enforce a law: death'., *New York Times*, 4 November 1992, sec. A, p. 22. Brooke, J., 'Head of Security in São Paulo is dismissed', *New York Times*, 9 October 1992, sec. A, p. 3.

114 US Department of State: *Brazil Country Report on Human Rights Practices for 1997*, http://www.state.gov/www/global/human_rights/1977_hrpreport/brazil.html.

115 www.1.1umm.edu/humanrts/instree/ainstls1.hm. My thanks to the interns at the Geonomics Center at Middlebury College, Vermont, who helped me locate the information on these treaties.

116 Ibid.

117 Father Ricardo Rezende Figueira, Rio Maria, Pará, 'Voloação dos Direitos Humanos dos camponeses no Brasil', paper presented to the 48th session of the Commission of Human Rights of the United Nations, 5 February 1992, Geneva, Switzerland.

118 Federal Constitution (1988) Law no. 7,716 (5 January 1989).

119 Law no. 9,459 signed by President Fernando Henrique Cardoso on 13 May 1997.

120 *Direitos Humanos no Cotidiano*, p. 87. Tape recorded interview with Luiz Mott, President Grupo Gay da Bahia, 4 July 1999.

121 *Raça Brasil*, July 1999.

122 *Raça Brasil*, June 1999.

123 *Raça Brasil*, September 1997.

124 See the case reprinted from the *Folha da Tarde* (São Paulo) 16 July 1991, reprinted in Guimarães, A.S.A. *Preconceito e Discriminação: Queixas de Ofensas e Tratamento Disigual dos Negros no Brasil*, Salvador, Bahia, Novos Toques, 1998, pp. 113–17. While doing research for this report, this author was stopped twice by policemen, once in Salvador and once in Rio de Janeiro, because he fitted the profile of supposed 'suspects'.

125 Roughly, 'very black person' and 'old black man'. I would like to acknowledge the help of Luiza Benicio of Salvador, Bahia, who helped me to understand these terms.

126 Depoimento, 'Nasce uma revolta...'., *Irohin* (Acompanhamento Legislativo, Executivo e Judiciáro), vol. 4, nos 4–5, pp. 2–3.

127 'Cartã Vermelha para a radialista gaúcho', *Raça Brasil*, October 1998, p. 98.

128 Guimarães, *op. cit.*, pp. 33–4.

129 Guimarães, *op. cit.*, pp. 43–64 and 100–1.

130 Human Rights Watch, *Final Justice: Police and Death Squad Homicides of Adolescents in Brazil*, New York, Washington, Los Angeles and London, 1994, pp. ix, 1–2.

131 Ibid., p. 3.

132 Ibid., pp. 13–22.

133 Mindlin, B., 'O Ministerio da Educação e a pluralidade cultural', *O Estado de São Paulo*, 27 October 1997.

NOTES

134 Lopez, I., 'A Flor da Pele: Pesquisa revela desprepar de profesores em lidar com as questões racias na escola', *Educação*, vol. 26, no. 218, pp. 20–2.

135 See Lima, H.P., *Histórias da Preta*, São Paulo, Companhia das Letrinhas, 1998.

136 Tape recorded interview with Maria Aparecida 'Cidinha' da Silva in the office of Generação XXI, São Paulo, Brazil, 30 June 1999.

137 'Generação XXI', *Educação*, June 1999, p. 22.

138 Hanchard, M.G., *Orpheus and Power: The Movimento Negro of Rio de Janeiro and São Paulo, Brazil, 1945–1988*, Princeton, NJ, Princeton University Press, 1994.

139 Tape recorded interview with Roseli Fischman, São Paulo, Brazil, 28 June 1999.

Andrews, George Reid, *Black People and White People in São Paulo, Brazil, 1888–1988*, Madison, University of Wisconsin Press, 1991.

Butler, Kim D., *Freedoms Given Freedoms Won: Afro-Brazilians in Post-Abolition São Paulo and Salvador*, New Brunswick, NJ, Rutgers University Press, 1998.

Da Costa, Emilia Viotti, *The Brazilian Empire: Myths and Histories*, Belmont, Wadsworth Publishing Company Inc., 1985.

Davis, Darién J. (ed.), *Slavery and Beyond: The African Impact on Latin America and the Caribbean*, Wilmington, Scholarly Resources, 1995.

Davis, Darién J., *Avoiding the Dark: Race and the Forging of National Culture in Modern Brazil*, Aldershot, Hants, Ashgate Publishing, 1999.

De Queirós Mattoso, Katia M., *To Be a Slave in Brazil, 1550–1880*, trans. Arthur Goldhammer, New Brunswick, NJ, Rutgers University Press, 1986.

Degler, Carl, *Neither Black nor White: Slavery and Race Relations in Brazil and the US*, New York, Macmillan, 1972.

Dzidzienyo, A. and Casal, L., *The Position of Black People in Brazilian and Cuban Society*, London, Minority Rights Group, 1979.

Fontaine, Pierre-Michel (ed.), *Race, Class and Power in Brazil*, Los Angeles, Center for Afro-American Studies UCLA, 1985.

Graham, Richard (ed.), *The Idea of Race in Latin America, 1870–1940*, Austin, University of Texas Press, 1990.

Hanchard, Michael George, *Orpheus and Power: The Movimento Negro of Rio de Janeiro and São Paulo, Brazil, 1945–1988*, Princeton, NJ, Princeton University Press, 1994.

Jackson, Richard L., *The Black Image in Latin American Literature*, Albuquerque, University of New Mexico, 1976.

Jesus, Maria Carolina de, *Child of the Dark*, New York, New American Library, 1962.

Levine, Robert M., *Father of the Poor? Vargas and his Era*, Cambridge, Cambridge University Press, 1998.

Levine, Robert M., Meihy, Bom and Sebe José Carlos, *The Life and Death of Carolina Maria de Jesus*, Alburquerque, University of New Mexico Press, 1995.

Minority Rights Group (ed.), *No Longer Invisible: Afro-Brazilians Today*, London, Minority Rights Group, 1995.

Nascimento, Abdias do, *Mixture or Massacre? Essays on the Genocide of a Black People*, trans. Elisa Larkin do Nascimento, New York, Afrodiaspora, 1979.

Nascimento, Abdias do and Nascimento, Elisa Larkin do, *Africans in Brazil: A Pan-African Perspective*, Trenton, NJ, Africa World Press, 1992.

Skidmore, Thomas, *Black into White: Race and Nationality in Brazilian Thought*, New York, Oxford University Press, 1974.